Advance Praise for *It's Not About You*

"*It's Not About You* reveals the secret that all truly great leaders know: genuine influence is about putting other people first."

—DAVID BACH, #1 *New York Times* bestselling author of *The Automatic Millionaire*

"Bob Burg and John David Mann have broken new ground in management literature. In the current global context, where the trust gap is widening in every aspect of business leadership, *It's Not About You* raises our consciousness to a new level, poignantly delivering the essence of leadership through an engaging story. On a personal note, I happened to read the manuscript during a critical juncture in my life, and I felt as if the book *held* me. It is now essential leadership reading for everyone at MindTree." —SUBROTO BAGCHI, Vice Chairman, MindTree Ltd.

"Genuine influence—not manipulation or power politics—is what makes the world go round, and this little book captures it beautifully, heart and soul."

—MADDY DYCHTWALD, cofounder, Age Wave, author of *Influence: How Women's Soaring Economic Power Will Transform Our World for the Better*

"A thoroughly enjoyable and educational exploration of the most powerful way to work successfully with others! I highly recommend it."

—TOM HOPKINS, author of *How to Master the Art of Selling* and *Selling in Tough Times*

"Burg and Mann have done it again! *It's Not About You* beautifully illustrates that the best way to have more in your life is to want more for others."

—JOHN JANTSCH, author of *Duct Tape Marketing* and *The Referral Engine*

"Burg and Mann are not just great storytellers, they are also men of heart and soul. *It's Not About You* is a gem of insight that reveals one of the true secrets to lasting business success."

—GARY KELLER, *New York Times* bestselling author of *The Millionaire Real Estate Agent* and *SHIFT: How Top Real Estate Agents Tackle Tough Times*

"This book reveals the simplest and most powerful secret you will discover in your lifetime. Digest its message and be the best leader you've ever known!"

   —DONNA KRECH, founder, Thin & Healthy Fitness Centers

"Another winner from Burg and Mann! *It's Not About You* communicates relevant and timely lessons on leadership and influence in an engaging story. You'll want to give this to your boss, your spouse, and every business person you know. They will thank you for the gift of a powerful lesson on empowering leadership."

   —MICHAEL J. MAHER, author of *(7L) The Seven Levels of Communication*

"*It's Not About You* touches the heart and shapes the mind. This powerful story of leadership will stay with you long after you turn the last page."

   —MOLLIE W. MARTI, PhD, JD, coauthor of *The 12 Factors of Business Success*

"*It's Not About You* will share space with *The Go-Giver* on a special bookshelf in my office labeled Must Read Twice—and there are fewer than ten books on that shelf. Bob and John have captured the very essence of what leads to generational or legacy success: sit in the other guy's chair first, care about their desires, and display personal integrity at all times."

   —FRANK McKINNEY, bestselling author of *The Tap*

"*It's Not About You* clearly conveys the crucial keys to business success through 'legendary leadership' and delivers them in a masterfully written, truly captivating story that you won't want to stop reading. Whether you're new to business or have been in business for years, this is likely to become the most valued, most utilized addition to your library of business books."

   —IVAN MISNER, *New York Times* bestselling author of *Masters of Networking* and founder, BNI® and Referral Institute®

"This entertaining and enlightening parable will give you the courage to succeed on your terms while supporting and inspiring the people around you. Highly recommended."

—**MICHAEL PORT**, *New York Times* bestselling author of *The Think Big Manifesto*

"*It's Not About You* is a beautiful meditation on the foundations of business and leadership. Enjoy the story—and then go apply its plentiful nuggets of wisdom in your work and life."

—**NIDO QUBEIN**, president, High Point University, and chairman, Great Harvest Bread

"This book gets to the heart of what really counts in business: character, caring, and a focus on others. I hope you enjoy this important 'little story' as much as I did!"   —**SCOTT ROOT**, President and CEO, Astra Tech, Inc.

"A captivating book, packed with *Aha!* moments. As with *The Go-Giver*, Burg and Mann draw you in and hold you with a powerful story that works on many levels at once. *It's Not About You* will delight you, surprise you, and move you. More than that, it will *change* you."

—**DONDI SCUMACI**, author *Designed for Success* and *Career Moves*

"The best in business get that it's not about them—it's about being useful to others. Read, study, and apply the ideas in this superb little gem of a book."

—**ROBIN SHARMA**, international bestselling author of *The Leader Who Had No Title*

"The message from this decade is that corporate leadership is broken. The message from this book is that business excellence cannot be achieved without ethics, humility, and trust. Read it, digest it, apply it, and watch your company flourish."

—**PAMELA SLIM**, author of *Escape from Cubicle Nation: From Corporate Prisoner to Thriving Entrepreneur*

"A breath of fresh air in the world of competing business books today."

—**SUSAN WILSON SOLOVIC**, author of *The Girls' Guide to Building a Million-Dollar Business*

"*It's Not About You* captures the true essence of leadership in a delightful parable that provides insight and encouragement throughout. The story's Five Keys to Legendary Leadership contain nuggets that will help anyone improve their effectiveness in managing and influencing people. I wholeheartedly recommend it to anyone willing to learn that it's not about you, but about those you lead."

   —**ARLIN SORENSEN, CEO**, Heartland Technology Solutions

"Burg and Mann have once again crafted a powerful story that touches our soul and encourages us all to grow. *It's Not About You* goes straight to the heart. It will change you forever."

   —**STEFAN SWANEPOEL**, *New York Times* bestselling author of *Surviving Your Serengeti: 7 Skills to Master Business and Life*

"This little gem is a cornucopia of big life lessons. Should be required reading for all college graduates!"

   —**DENIS WAITLEY**, bestselling author of *The Seeds of Greatness*

"They've done it again! As someone who recommends *The Go-Giver* to every business owner I meet, I didn't think there would ever be a title to compare. I was wrong. Now, I'm suggesting *two* must-reads! I read *It's Not About You* from cover to cover, captivated by Ben and Aunt Elle. If you are in business, or even hope to have an ounce of influence in your life's work, get this book, read it and then *live* it."

   —**CARRIE WILKERSON**, author of *The Barefoot Executive*

"In today's leadership desert of self-centered actions, people yearn for the oasis of principle-based servant leadership, a model masterfully portrayed by Bob Burg and John David Mann in their new book, *It's Not About You*. Don't just read this book: more importantly, learn it, live it, and share it!"

   —**ORRIN WOODWARD**, *New York Times* bestselling coauthor of *Launching a Leadership Revolution*

IT'S
NOT ABOUT
YOU

IT'S
NOT ABOUT
YOU

A Little Story About

What Matters Most in Business

Bob Burg

and

John David Mann

Portfolio / Penguin

PORTFOLIO / PENGUIN
Published by the Penguin Group
Penguin Group (USA) Inc., 375 Hudson Street, New York, New York 10014, U.S.A.
Penguin Group (Canada), 90 Eglinton Avenue East, Suite 700, Toronto, Ontario, Canada M4P 2Y3
(a division of Pearson Penguin Canada Inc.)
Penguin Books Ltd, 80 Strand, London WC2R 0RL, England
Penguin Ireland, 25 St. Stephen's Green, Dublin 2, Ireland (a division of Penguin Books Ltd)
Penguin Books Australia Ltd, 250 Camberwell Road, Camberwell, Victoria 3124, Australia
(a division of Pearson Australia Group Pty Ltd)
Penguin Books India Pvt Ltd, 11 Community Centre, Panchsheel Park,
New Delhi – 110 017, India
Penguin Group (NZ), 67 Apollo Drive, Rosedale, Auckland 0632, New Zealand
(a division of Pearson New Zealand Ltd)
Penguin Books (South Africa) (Pty) Ltd, 24 Sturdee Avenue,
Rosebank, Johannesburg 2196, South Africa

Penguin Books Ltd, Registered Offices: 80 Strand, London WC2R 0RL, England

First published in 2011 by Portfolio / Penguin, a member of Penguin Group (USA) Inc.

1   3   5   7   9   10   8   6   4   2

LIBRARY OF CONGRESS CATALOGING IN PUBLICATION DATA
Burg, Bob.
It's not about you : a little story about what matters most in business / Bob Burg and
John David Mann.
p. cm.
ISBN 978-1-59184-419-8
1. Success in business. I. Mann, John David. II. Title.
HF5386.B8883 2011
658.4'09—dc22   2011013962

Printed in the United States of America

To Mike and Myrna Burg

and Ana Gabriel Mann:

You hold us up.

CONTENTS

1

THE OFFER

B en emerged from the parking garage, blinking in the bright September sunlight. "You've got this, Ben," he murmured as he set off down the street. "This is going to be a piece of cake."

He arrived at the address he'd been given, a sturdy old brick building that took up half the city block. He squinted and looked up. There it was, inscribed on a large brass plate riveted onto the brick facing above the entrance:

ALLEN & AUGUSTINE

MAKERS AND MARKETERS OF FINE CHAIRS

"It'll be a piece of cake," he repeated as he stepped through the gigantic oak doors and into the foyer, where he was greeted by the scent of wood shavings, leather, and varnish.

Allen & Augustine had fallen on hard times. That was why Ben was here.

Ben had a reputation as someone who did his homework, ran hard, and knew how to go in for the kill. He'd closed accounts by the score, individual clients by the hundreds. There were some who said he might be executive material.

Still, he'd never faced a situation quite like this before.

The conference room was filled with some two dozen people milling about and talking in hushed tones. Ben was the only outsider. He moved through the group, shaking hands, meeting the members of Allen & Augustine's executive team and exploratory committee.

As he reached the head of the table he saw two chairs and, standing by them, Allen & Augustine's two co-chairmen.

He was introduced first to a slender, soft-spoken gentleman—Allen, co-founder of the company, who greeted Ben quietly—and then the barrel-chested man standing next to him, who gave Ben a warm welcome and a two-fisted handshake: Allen's brother, Augustine.

Next he met a burly man with tree-trunk hands: Frank, VP of Production. Frank said not a word, giving only a terse nod.

Finally Ben was introduced to the VP of Finance and Personnel, Karen, a petite woman with intelligent dark eyes. "So this is Ben," she said. Ben couldn't quite decide whether she seemed hostile or just cautious.

If he could successfully influence these four executives, Ben knew he'd have the company. He had to win them over. To convince them.

In a word, to *conquer* them.

"Let's not kid ourselves," he'd muttered to his reflection in the mirror that morning while shaving. "This is a battlefield."

In his twelve years with the Marden Group, Ben had moved from sales to sales management to division manager. Now, at the tender age of thirty-four, he had been promoted to a position—on probation—in the firm's highly competitive Mergers & Acquisitions department.

Ben's task was to lead the transition—"a *smooth* transition," as the boss had emphasized when giving Ben the job just three days earlier—with this newly acquired company, helping them become a successful, productive part of the Marden Group. One big, happy family.

Except that the newly acquired company wasn't actually acquired yet.

And that was Ben's charge: to persuade the owners of Allen & Augustine that this merger was in their best interests. And because all of Allen & Augustine's roughly five hundred employees had been given generous employee-stock-ownership plans, they *were* the owners. All Ben had to do was persuade five hundred people to lay down their arms, so to speak, and see things his way.

No, he'd never faced a situation quite like this before.

The babble in the room quieted to a hush as everyone took their seats. After a brief introduction, Allen turned the floor over to Ben.

"Makers and marketers," Ben began slowly, deliberately, as he got to his feet, "of fine chairs. All made of premium wood, all hand-designed, all exquisite. 'When you sit in an Allen & Augustine chair,'" he was now quoting from their ads, "'you don't just feel supported, you feel *held*.'"

In fact, that was the company's slogan: *We hold you up.* Ben couldn't help thinking what a hokey motto that was.

"Tiny chairs for tots, tykes, and nursery nooks," he continued. "Big, bold boardroom chairs. Classic country kitchen chairs, elegant straight-back dining room chairs, cozy deep-cushioned chairs for grandparents, comfy rockers for nursing moms. The chairs that held a generation."

Ben noticed the body language in the room as people stiffly shifted position. *Not good.*

"From what I understand, half our city council were fed, burped, and rocked to sleep in Allen & Augustine chairs." He paused for a fraction of a second, then added, "And that was just this past weekend."

This got a decent laugh from around the table. *Good.*

"All hand-designed, all exquisite," he repeated, pacing slowly as he spoke. "That's how your catalog describes your wares. And you know what? It's also a fitting description of your company.

"You are, as you all know, a legend in this city.

"The entire business community appreciates what a tight-knit company you have here. Many of your employees have been here from the start, or at least the early days, and I understand there are even a good number of second-generation employees.

"It's no secret that Allen & Augustine has been one of the city's great success stories.

"*But . . .*"

Ben had learned to wield the word *but* like a cutlass, using it to slice through his opponents' most potent premises and propositions. Sometimes he used it slyly, like a concealed trap door; at other times it had all the subtlety of a hand grenade.

Like now.

He glanced around the room to see how he was doing.

"*But,*" he repeated, "let's face facts. Times have been tough. Overseas competition is fierce, costs are up, sales are down, profits are getting squeezed.

"Your executives have refused to let go a single employee, and I admire that. Instead you've been forced to implement pay cuts across the board. I know you're hurting." He paused—then added: "I'm here to help the bleeding stop."

He had practiced this line for hours over the weekend. He didn't want to sound patronizing. And besides, he meant it. It was painful to see this once great company brought to its knees, and as far as he was concerned, his employer was exactly the white knight these people needed.

But how to convince *them* of that?

"I want you to know," he continued, "that the Marden Group knows what it means to be a family business. We *are* one.

"You probably know our story. Founded in New York in the 1930s by Andrew Marden, an immigrant merchant turned industrialist and land speculator. Old man Marden passed the business on to his daughter, Elizabeth, who married into the Bushnell family and, after running the company successfully for many years, eventually passed the mantle on to her son, the founder's grandson, our current president and CEO, Thomas J. Bushnell."

Ben had actually seen Thomas J., live and in person, just twice in his life. The first time had been twelve years earlier, Ben's first year at Marden, when the boss had put in an appearance at a divisional retreat. The second time was last Friday—just three short days ago—when he had summoned Ben to his office.

In that brief meeting, Mr. Bushnell had made clear how much he wanted this deal to happen. The competition in Mergers & Acquisitions was fierce, all right, and if Ben didn't get this one right, there were any number of equally ambitious executives nipping at his heels.

Ben's job, and his and Melanie's future, were on the line here.

"At this point," declared the boss, "the wind over there at Allen & Augustine could blow just as easily one way as the other. And which way it *does* end up blowing is going to come down to one thing." He had looked straight at Ben as he concluded their interview with a final word. "You."

Ben drew a breath. Here it was.

"As you know," he told the assembled group, "Mr. Bushnell and the Marden Group have tendered an offer to purchase Allen & Augustine.

"Over the next few days I'll be meeting with your founders and top department heads, and getting to know you and your employees.

"Next Monday, one week from today, you have a very important meeting—possibly *the* most important meeting in your company's history. At that meeting, you and all your employees will be asked to answer a question with one of two words.

"Yes. Or no."

He glanced around the table.

Ben was pretty good at judging the sense of a room, and right now he had the sense that these people were tilting his way. If he could demonstrate that even a third of those present were leaning toward "yes," it would spell certain victory for him. Eight *yeas* would be an ample number to make the others doubt their *nay* positions. Hey, even *six* on his side would do it. It was a gamble, but he was feeling solid.

He leaned forward, one hand on the table, and struck a more casual posture.

"Tell you what," he said. "Just to get a sense of where we are, let's take a preliminary show of hands. Nothing in stone, but just informally . . ." Ben began lifting his own hand as he spoke: "How many of us would be inclined to vote yes right now?"

Not one hand went up.

Over the next ten minutes, as the meeting broke and Ben mingled politely before heading out of the conference room, down the elevator, and out onto the street, just one thought played in his mind.

This was not going to be a piece of cake.

2

THE QUESTION

Leaving the old brick building behind, Ben headed down the street to a little restaurant around the corner that a friend had told him about. It was her favorite place, she'd said, and if he was ever in that part of town, he *had* to try it.

He entered the jam-packed café and, sure enough, there was his friend, sitting at a corner table. He had sort of hoped he might bump into her here. In fact, that was his plan.

Claire was a sought-after marketing expert who had done some freelance work for Allen & Augustine a few years back, before landing her current cherry position as director of fundraising for a big local nonprofit that had its offices nearby. It had occurred to Ben that Claire might be able to give him some valuable intel on the place, maybe illuminate the internal politics—who called the shots and who held the power cards.

It never hurt to have the inside scoop.

Ben was just about to get Claire's attention when he saw, to his chagrin, that she was not alone: across the table from her sat an elderly woman, fussing with a pot of hot tea. He was just debating whether to stay or leave when Claire glanced over and spotted him by the door.

"Ben!" she called out, and waved him over.

"Ben, I want you to meet Aunt Elle." Ah, thought Ben as Claire made the introductions and he shook the woman's hand. Her face had looked vaguely familiar, and that explained it. *Family resemblance.*

At that moment a waiter came over with a small tray: coffee for Claire, a rich-looking dessert for her aunt. "Stay and join us," said Claire. "We have to go soon, but you can keep our table."

As her companion dipped into her dessert, Claire turned to Ben.

"What brings you to this part of town?"

Ben briefly explained, sketching the situation in broad strokes. He did not mention the name of the company he'd been visiting, only that it was a well-established manufacturing firm that had fallen on hard times, and that the Marden Group was making an offer. He didn't want to go into too much detail just yet. The walls, after all, had ears.

Aunt Elle piped up. "So you're with the Marden Group?"

Yes, Ben told her, he was. "You've heard of them?"

Aunt Elle nodded vaguely, then turned her attention back to her zabaglione and hot tea.

Ben told Claire briefly what he was up against.

"So I've got a week," he concluded, "to bring five hundred people around to my way of thinking." He paused. "Any ideas?"

Claire frowned in thought for a moment, then—to Ben's surprise—turned to her companion and said, "I don't know. Aunt Elle? What would you suggest?"

Ben groaned inwardly.

Aunt Elle looked up at Ben. "These people you have to persuade—five, you said?"

"Five *hundred*, actually," Ben gently corrected.

"Of course. These people, then, they don't agree with your picture of things?"

"Not yet," replied Ben. "Which is exactly why I have to *convince* them."

She pursed her lips, then said, "Well." She leaned toward him to give her next words emphasis.

"*The less you say, the more influence you'll have.*"

Ben nodded thoughtfully in an effort to be polite.

"Do you know why that is?" she added.

"No, I don't," replied Ben. "Why?"

"Because the more you yield, the more power you have."

Ben shot a glance at Claire, hoping to steer the conversation back her way, but she was focused on her coffee and, from what Ben could see, stifling a giggle.

Ben had to say something, or risk appearing rude.

"That sounds . . . very Zen."

Claire's giggle escaped. "He's right!" she said. "I'll have to start calling you Aunt Zen!"

Aunt Elle cocked an eyebrow at them both, then returned once more to her zabaglione.

"So, Claire . . ." Ben began. "Can I ask you a favor?"

"Name it," said Claire.

"I'm meeting with the key people there, tomorrow morning and for the rest of the week. I could use the expert objectivity of a friend here. If you have any time, I'd love to get your take on those meetings. Sort of a . . . debriefing." *Intel. The inside scoop.*

Claire set her coffee down, glanced at Aunt Elle, then down at the cup, and then up at Ben. She seemed to be weighing some conflicting considerations in her mind. Finally, she nodded.

"Okay," she said. "I can't promise I'll give you any great insights. But sure. Why don't we meet right here for lunch tomorrow?"

The waiter brought the ladies' bill, and as Claire took care of it, Aunt Elle suddenly spoke up again. "May I ask you a question?"

"Of course."

"These five people—you say you've made them an offer?"

"Five *hundred*," Ben prompted.

"Yes, yes, five hundred."

She looked up at Ben and fixed him with a gaze. He was surprised he had not noticed before how clear her ice-blue eyes were.

"What do you really have to offer them?"

She spoke the words with a librarian's hushed directness, as Ben imagined she might have shushed thousands of unruly pupils over the decades. *You—no talking!* He felt momentarily rattled.

"Well," he stammered, "we bring significant resources to the table," and he began going through an explanation of the advantages that come from economies of scale, distribution channels, market footprint, and so forth. He finished his paragraph, aware that for some reason it all rang rather hollow, and thought, Why am I feeling defensive, explaining myself to a person I don't even know?!

Aunt Elle waited until he had finished, then nodded and said, "Ah."

Ben felt as if he'd been back in grade school taking a pop quiz . . . and had flunked.

———

That night, as Ben told Melanie about his day, he described the conversation with Claire and how he'd met her librarian aunt.

"And then she asks me the nuttiest question," he told her. "She says, *'What do you really have to offer them?'* Just like that. I couldn't believe it."

Melanie looked at Ben thoughtfully. After a moment she said, "Hang on," and left the room. She came back with a small gift-wrapped package and handed it to him.

"I got you something. It's a woo-hoo-sweetheart, congratulations-on-your-promotion-to-Mergers-and-Acquisitions gift."

Ben took it from her hand and carefully unwrapped it. It was a beautifully bound notebook. On the cover, in hand-lettered calligraphy, Melanie had inscribed:

Ben's Manifesto

"Go on, open it," she said. He turned the cover and opened the book to the first page. Although the rest of the volume was entirely blank, Melanie had written a title atop the very first page, consisting of five words:

Ben's Keys to Legendary Leadership

"Really," he said. "Legendary leadership? You think that's maybe stretching just a little, Mel? I'm a probie at Mergers & Acquisitions. That's not exactly chairman of the Joint Chiefs of Staff."

She grinned and punched him in the shoulder. "Yes, my general." Then she nodded at the book and said, "Read the inscription."

He looked at the inside cover and saw six words written there:

For Ben—I believe in you.

He looked back at Mel. How had he been so lucky to find her—
and to get *her* to say yes all those years ago?

"Well, I do," she said.

Ben stuck his hands in his pockets and pulled them inside out.
"I hate to break it to you," he said, "but I don't seem to be holding
any keys to anything but the car."

"You will," she said. She lapsed into silence, and seemed to be
mulling something over.

"Mel?" said Ben.

"Mmm? Oh, nothing. I was just thinking."

"And . . . ?" coaxed Ben. This was something he loved about
Mel. She really *thought* about things.

"Well," said Melanie. "It's just—what the old lady said. What
do you think?"

"I think she's a little batty," Ben replied with a grin.

"No, I mean her question. What you have to offer these people.
What do you think?"

He shook his head, not so much to say no as to shake off the
question. "C'mon, Mel. What kind of question is that?"

That night Ben lay awake long after Melanie had fallen asleep,
staring at the ceiling.

What *did* he really have to offer them?

3

THE TOP FLOOR

Bright the next morning, Ben entered the sturdy old brick building, steaming coffee in hand, on his way to engage the enemy. Later on, after lunch, he would meet with some of the employees. First up, though, was a meeting with Allen, co-founder and co-chair, who served as co-president and head of Planning.

This was strategic. Like Achilles going to do battle with Hector on the fields of Troy, Ben figured hand-to-hand combat was a lot smarter than trying to take on the entire army. And on a one-on-one footing, he felt pretty confident. Ben had closed a *lot* of sales in his day.

Bypassing the front desk, he entered one of the old elevators and pressed 8—the building's top floor.

The moment Ben walked into Allen's office, the slender man rose from his desk.

"Ben," said Allen, beckoning as he stepped over to the solid plate-glass wall behind him. "Let me show you something."

Ben joined him and gazed out at the view. The day outside was crisp, the view crystal. Ben could see clear across the city and beyond to the long, rolling range of mountains in the west.

"You know why my office is on the top floor?"

"To remind everyone that you're the boss?"

Allen laughed. He pointed into the distance. "See that narrow valley, way over there?" Ben saw it. "Augustine and I grew up there."

He pointed a few degrees to the north, where Ben saw a richly forested area. "Over there? That's where we started our first timber-management program.

"When we bought this building, some fifteen years ago, I had this entire section of wall pulled out and plate glass installed in its place, so I could see what you're seeing right now, every single day.

"For anyone who wants to lead any kind of organization, I think that may be *the* most important thing."

Ben didn't follow. "What's that?"

Allen looked over at Ben briefly. "To never forget where you came from." He returned his gaze to the distant valley.

"We started the business right near there, out of an old abandoned church. With some friends' help, we were able to pick it up at auction for a song. It was about to be torn down."

" '*The stone the builders rejected, it has become the cornerstone,*' eh?" commented Ben.

Allen smiled and nodded. "Pretty much."

"You mentioned a timber-management program?"

In truth, Ben already knew all about this. In the four days since being given this assignment, he had done a ton of research on this company, or at least as much as he could pull off in a few days. But he wanted to hear about it from Allen's perspective.

"Well," said Allen. "You're looking at the trees that make our chairs. Of course, not all our stock grows right there"—he waved a hand across the panoramic view—"but most of it comes from a few hundred miles around. We use only woods sourced from managed forests, to preserve and protect the trees. Because of our aggressive planting program, we actually have a net *positive* impact on the nation's forests.

"It's expensive. But necessary. And it's this"—he swept his hand across the scene again—"that won't let me forget."

"How does that work out for you, financially?"

Allen gave Ben another brief glance. "As I said, it's expensive. People laughed at us when we started. But we believed customers would be willing to pay. And it turned out, we had the last laugh, because they were." Now he turned to look at Ben. "Did you know that by year three, we were written up in the city's annual *Best of . . .* guide as the most—"

"The most promising new startup in the city?"

Allen gave a short laugh and a brief salute. "You do your homework."

Ben smiled. "I wasn't kidding yesterday when I said you guys are one of the city's great success stories."

This was a subtle move on Ben's part. Both he and Allen knew that when he had made that statement in the Allen & Augustine boardroom the day before, his next word had been "*But . . .*"

Allen nodded and turned back to the view.

"There's something else I see out here."

"The city?" ventured Ben.

Allen gave another short laugh. "Well, you can hardly help seeing that, no matter where you stand. But no, I meant the mountains.

"The forests remind me what we're doing. The mountains remind me why we're doing it. The incredible heights we're capable of. The greatness.

"The view out there is magnificent on its own," he added, "but what makes it important to me is that it feeds the view in here," and he tapped one finger to his forehead. "And this in here—this is the view that makes everything else happen out there."

For a moment he said nothing, just gazed out at the western peaks. Then he inhaled, let out a big breath, and turned to face Ben.

"Please, sit."

He ushered Ben to a plain-looking wooden chair in front of his desk. Ben sat—and was stunned at the sensation.

He felt as if he were suspended in a harness that had been perfectly custom-fitted to the exact contours of his back and thighs. It was almost unearthly, like an astronaut floating in space. He felt . . . *held*.

"Whoa!" he said.

Allen smiled and nodded. "Never sat in one of our custom chairs before, have you?"

Ben shook his head.

"That's the first," Allen said.

"Yes," Ben admitted, "it's a first for me."

"No," said Allen, "I mean, it's *the* first. That's the very first chair we made, twenty-eight years ago."

Ben leapt from the chair as if it were on fire and scrambled to his feet. "Omigosh!"

"It's okay!" said Allen, laughing. "Don't worry. It's historic, but definitely not fragile." His smile faded as he added this afterthought: "I'd love to be able to say the same thing about the business itself."

There was an awkward silence for a moment.

Ben settled back into the First Chair, and Allen took his own seat behind the big desk.

"Well," Ben began, "that's, of course, why I'm here. I want to see Allen & Augustine recapture its former glory—"

"So do I, Ben," said Allen, "so do I. But I have to tell you straight—I am *not* in favor of this merger. I'm sure the folks at the Marden Group are all very well-meaning people. But being well-meaning, even well-funded, is not enough."

He swiveled his chair again to gaze out through the expanse of plate glass.

"You don't have this view."

Ben weighed his options. He felt he had somewhat lost control of the conversation. Should he try to regain the upper hand and go for the close now, or give the man some room to regroup his thoughts?

He was about to launch his carefully rehearsed argument when Allen started speaking again.

"You can't see that old church from here," said Allen, "because it's not there anymore. One summer night, that third year in business—in fact, soon after that *Best of* article came out—a fire started. No one knows how. It raged out of control. Burned all our inventory and raw materials, every file and account record—and those were the days when *all* our records were still on paper.

"Nobody was hurt. But after a two-day blaze, our business was literally in ashes. Everything but that one chair, which, as it happened, was not on the premises at the time." He nodded at the chair Ben was sitting in. "Just the week before, we'd presented it as a gift to the master craftsman who taught us the art of woodworking. After the fire he insisted on giving it back to us."

Allen gave a quiet laugh. "That's ironic, isn't it? The only reason we still have that chair," he mused, "is that we gave it away."

Ben nodded. "I read about that fire. It must have been awful."

"It gets worse," said Allen. "There was a problem with our in-surance. The fire wasn't covered."

"You're kidding!" This tragic tidbit was one thing Ben's research had *not* uncovered.

"Nope," said Allen. "Total wipeout."

"Wow" was all Ben could think to say.

"Indeed."

"So what did you do?"

Allen swiveled back to look at Ben.

"That evening, after the fire trucks left, I gathered the entire group—there were about twenty of us back then—out in the front yard and asked them, 'You know why this place burned down?'

" 'Karma?' said one person, which managed to get a laugh from the others. 'Arson,' said another. 'Really *really* bad luck,' said a third." Allen gave a rueful smile. "They were pretty down. And who could blame them?"

He glanced out at the view again, then back at Ben.

"I turned and pointed up toward the city skyline in the distance. It was dusk. All the lights were starting to flicker on. And I said:

" *'Because it was time to move to a bigger building.'*

"The building I pointed at was the building you and I are sitting in right now."

Ben was mesmerized. For the moment, he had completely forgotten that he was here to win this man over.

"Of course," Allen continued, "it wasn't that simple. It took another ten years to get from that point to where we actually acquired this place. And it nearly didn't happen—a dozen times, a hundred times. It's easy to inspire and motivate people—for the moment. It's easy to say, 'Hold a vision.' You know what the hard part is?"

Ben shook his head.

"The hard part isn't the *vision*. Anyone can come up with a vision. The hard part is the *holding*."

The *holding*. Ben thought about that.

"Sure," continued Allen, "everyone was inspired and motivated that evening in the churchyard, and the next day, too. But within a week, most were ready to quit. Again, who could blame them? We had no money, no inventory, no plant, nothing. What I told our group, standing by the ruins of our burnt-out church, was a flat-out absurdity on the face of it. There was absolutely no evidence that it could possibly happen. We had to move forward on invisible wires, without a net.

"And that's what it's all about, Ben. Building a business takes skill, work, and materials . . . but those are details. More than anything else, building a business—really, building *anything*—is an act of faith. Because you're creating something out of nothing, you see?"

Ben simply nodded.

"Here's what they don't teach you about leadership in business school, Ben.

"The single biggest challenge to any organization is the constant cloud of fear and doubt that swirls around the heads of the people involved. As a leader, your job is to hold fast to the big picture, to keep seeing in your mind's eye, with crystal clarity, where it is you're going—that place that right at this moment exists *only* in your mind's eye. And to *keep* seeing that, even when nobody else does.

"*Especially* when nobody else does.

"Your people count on you to do this. It's the biggest job you have."

Allen had been looking out at his view the entire time he was speaking, but now he turned again and faced Ben.

"Every challenge we've faced, every time we've been in a scrape, what has gotten us through it is . . ." He leaned forward and gently tapped one forefinger to Ben's forehead.

"*Seeing.*"

4

INFLUENCE

When Ben entered the crowded café this time, the maître d', a big man named Sal, recognized him at once. "This way, sir," he said with a small bow, and he ushered Ben to the same corner table as the day before. As he approached, Ben saw that Claire was already seated—and that, once again, her aunt was with her. His heart sank.

"You sure I'm not imposing?" he said, standing at the table tentatively. "Maybe you two have your own stuff to talk about?"

In truth, he really didn't want to be grilled by Aunt Elle again today. He had hoped to talk privately with just Claire.

"Don't be silly," said Claire. "We were expecting you. Weren't we, Aunt Elle?"

The older lady looked at Ben with an unreadable expression. Annoyance? Amusement? I'm sure she was a good librarian, thought Ben, but she would've made a *great* poker player.

Ben took his seat just as a young waiter came by to take their order. Once their lunch orders were in, Ben briefly described his meeting with Allen (without mentioning his name) and how, despite the man's resistance to the merger, Ben had sensed he was worried about his company's fate.

"Do you think you were able to influence him at all?" asked Claire.

"I don't know," said Ben. "No . . . I'm sure I didn't convince him, not yet—but I think I can. The way I see it"—he felt himself warming to the topic—"what I'm offering him is exactly what the company needs to pull out of their slump. I really believe this is the right move for them—I can see it, I can taste it, I can smell it! No doubt in my mind, and if I can just convince him to listen to me, I'm *positive* we can turn this thing around."

Ben flashed on a mental picture of Allen standing in the burnt-out churchyard, pointing into the distance like Babe Ruth claiming his next home run, and he felt a bit of kinship. Truth be told, he was feeling a little inspired and motivated himself right now.

"This may seem an odd question." It was Aunt Elle who interrupted his thoughts. "Do you know roughly how many personal pronouns you just used?"

Ben looked at Aunt Elle, bewildered. "I'm sorry?"

"You know what a pronoun is," she said. "*He, she, you, me, us, them?*"

Ben nodded. "Sure. I mean, of course."

"You know why they're called *personal* pronouns?"

Ben shook his head.

"Because they're *personal*. In that little soliloquy you just gave, which was very nice, by the way, you said *I, me,* and *my* fifteen times."

Ben felt himself blush. At the same time, he couldn't help wondering, How did she *do* that? How had she kept count so accurately? Maybe she'd put in time as an English teacher as well as a librarian.

"Fifteen," he mumbled. "Really."

"Yes," she said brightly, "and you used the words *us* and *we*, well, let's see . . ." She cocked her head for a moment, as if replaying a recording of Ben's speech in her head, then said, "Ah, just once."

Ben didn't know what to say.

"So," she continued, "what kind of *metamessage* do you imagine that sends?"

"Metamessage?"

"Yes, the message underneath the message. My father used to say, 'Elle, when a boy starts talking to you, don't trust the lyrics—listen to the music.'"

Ben was lost. How had he gotten into this crazy conversation?

"There's what you say," Aunt Elle continued, "and then there's what you mean. For example, Claire asked you if you thought you had *influenced* the man you met with. You replied that you thought you could *convince* him. See?"

Ben was not sure he did.

"*Influence. Convince.* Two very different things."

"No offense," said Ben, "but isn't that just semantics?"

"Exactly!" she exclaimed. "That's absolutely what it is. And semantics counts. Semantics is incredibly powerful. You know what the word *semantic* means?"

Ben had to admit, now that he thought about it, that he did not.

"Basically, it means *what the word means*."

"Aunt Elle has this thing for the meaning of words," Claire confided to Ben. He had already guessed as much.

"You know what they say about the pen?" Aunt Elle said.

"That it's mightier than the sword?" ventured Ben.

"Yes—although that's not quite true. A pen is just a pen. It's not the pen that's mighty, it's the words you *write* with the pen. Words are the most powerful invention human beings have ever created."

Ben thought for a moment. "Hang on, though. Yesterday you said, 'The less you say, the more influence you'll have.'"

Aunt Elle pushed her glasses up on her nose and peered through them at Ben.

"You were listening. I am impressed."

Ben's face went red again. *Good grief*, he thought, *I'm blushing like a schoolgirl.*

"So," Aunt Elle continued, "may I ask another question?"

Ben simply nodded.

"If you want to influence these people, what is it you're actually trying to create there? That is, what *is* influence?"

"Influence? Uhh . . ." Ben grappled to come up with a clear definition. "Your ability to get people to do what you want them to?"

Aunt Elle frowned. "No, I mean, what *is* it? What is it *made* of?"

Ben had no idea how to even begin answering that one. He glanced helplessly at Claire, and saw that same suppressed giggle on her face. No help there.

"I give up," he said to Aunt Elle.

"Well," she said, hitching forward eagerly in her seat, "the word *influence* means *an unseen flow of power.* It was first used in the Middle Ages, believe it or not, as an astrological term, from an old French word meaning *a streaming ethereal power from the stars acting upon our character or destiny.* Imagine that!

"By the fifteenth century, the word was being used to mean

an exercise of personal power by human beings. You could say, it describes how we exert gravitational force on each other. Like stars."

"Okay . . ." Ben had no idea where she was going with this.

"So influence is a *flow*, like air flow or the flow of a river—and they both come from the same root word, by the way. So what creates that flow? When water pours downstream, is there some force pushing it?"

"Pushing it?" Ben thought for a moment. "No, it flows downstream because of gravity."

Aunt Elle nodded gravely. "Exactly. Look at it this way. Imagine you have an ordinary window fan, blowing air into your room. How far can it blow?"

Ben pictured what she was describing. "Not very far?"

"Not very far at all. But reverse the fan's position so it's now blowing outward—and you can *pull* a column of air from a single open window clear on the other side of the house, even hundreds of yards away.

"Or, think of it this way: How far can you *push* a rope?"

Ben felt lost again.

"You see? *That's* what influence is made of. That's what gravity does. That's what stars do—they *pull*. That's why we don't talk about how much *push* we might have with someone, but rather, how much *pull*.

"*Pull* is the substance of influence. Not *push*."

Ben thought about this for a long minute while Aunt Elle finished her tea.

Finally he said, "Which is why you said, 'The less you say, the more influence you'll have'?"

Aunt Elle turned to him, and, while he wasn't sure, he thought he detected the slightest hint of a smile playing at the edges of her mouth.

"Touché," she said.

After Aunt Elle left to take a taxi to an appointment, Ben said to Claire, "Your aunt is quite a character."

Claire laughed. "She's not really my aunt. That's just what I call her. She's a good friend. My mentor."

Ben nearly choked on his coffee. "Mentor?!"

"In her day, she was a very successful businesswoman," said Claire. "*Very* successful. Spends most of her time these days in charitable ventures. She's big into the local food bank and national feed-the-hungry campaigns. That, and literacy. Those are her two big passions: making sure people can eat, and that they can read. Feed their stomachs, she says, and feed their minds, and everything else will pretty well take care of itself. . . ."

Ben had missed most of this. He was still trying to wrap his mind around four words Claire had said a moment ago: *mentor* and *very successful businesswoman*.

Obviously, he was wrong about Aunt Elle being a librarian.

Maybe he was wrong about a few others things, too.

Maybe it wasn't Claire he was here to see. Maybe it was her crazy librarian aunt—no, scratch that: her crazy *very successful businesswoman* aunt. Who wasn't really her aunt after all . . . and maybe wasn't so crazy.

That night Ben sat at the little desk in his study, took out the notebook Melanie had given him, and opened it to the first page.

Ben's Keys to Legendary Leadership

"Here goes nothing," he muttered. "Let the legend begin." Humming the first few bars of the theme from *Superman*, he added a new line below the title Melanie had so carefully lettered:

KEY #1: HOLD THE VISION

He sat back and thought about his day, then turned to a new blank page and began to write:

HOLD THE VISION

Lead with your mind.

Anyone can come up with a vision.
The hard part is the holding.

Building a business—building anything—is an act of faith.

*Keep seeing in your mind's eye where it is you're going, even when
nobody else does. Especially when nobody else does.*

Never forget where you came from.

He paused, then added one more line toward the bottom of the
page:

And watch your personal pronouns.

5

THE HEART
OF THE OPERATION

Wednesday morning, when Ben asked the young man at the front desk for directions to Augustine's office, the fellow said, "Oh, you'll probably find him somewhere in Service. That's floors two through seven."

"Two through seven?!" Ben wasn't sure he'd heard this right. "But . . . that's practically every floor in the building!"

The young man grinned and said, "You want me to page him?"

Ben waved his hand dismissively as he turned away from the front desk. "I can find my way."

As he headed toward the bank of elevators, he overheard the young man mutter to another employee, "That's the guy who says we're such a great company, *but* . . ."

It was not lost on Ben that, while the employees were all being polite to his face, the currents of suspicion ran deep.

He pressed UP—and before the elevator door even opened, there came Augustine lumbering down the hall toward him. "Hey, hey! How's our corporate raider doing this morning!"

"Uh—" and before he'd figured out how to respond to *that*, Ben found himself wrapped in a big bear hug.

Ding! The elevator doors flew open and Augustine stepped in, pulling Ben in after him and punching the 2 button as he spoke. "C'mon, c'mon, I'll show you the operation."

The contrast between the two brothers could not have been greater. Where Allen was reflective and soft-spoken, even a bit reserved, Augustine was as warm and effusive as anyone Ben had ever met.

As they walked the brightly lit main hallway on the second floor, Ben noticed that every wall was generously decked out with photo spreads, all of them apparently depicting family events of different sizes, from intimate picnics to parties of dozens.

When the hall opened into an oversize foyer, Ben saw that the photo-spread motif continued, now with each large wall devoted to a different topic. Augustine narrated each one as they walked.

One wall was all wedding photos, another all pictures of children. A third was covered with photos of animals, each with its name scrawled on a caption at the bottom—crayon, ink, pencil, watercolor; Ben even saw one carefully lettered in colored chalk—and framed in glass to prevent smudging. These were the kids' pets, Augustine told him proudly, their names carefully inscribed by their respective humans.

"What do you think of our employee scrapbook?"

"It's . . . wild" was Ben's reply. It was like walking through a museum gallery, only this was a museum dedicated to everyday life. "Do you really take up six floors just for Customer Service?"

"Just *Service*," Augustine corrected. "We don't make a distinction. Customers, employees, employees' families, the community . . . It's all just Service."

He led Ben through a door that opened into a huge clear-span space filled with workbenches that were loaded with chairs and pieces of chairs, in every state of disassembly and disrepair.

"This is Repair, which is of course part of Service. Every Allen & Augustine chair carries a lifetime guarantee. Your chair breaks, or gets wobbly, you send it to us. We pay shipping. We fix it and ship it back—no charge to you."

Ben was well aware of Allen & Augustine's famous guarantee. He was tempted to say, "No wonder you're going broke," but he held his tongue.

"Crazy, huh?" Augustine laughed. "I know. That's what they all said when we first put the policy in place. That was twenty-eight years ago. Now everyone's copying us."

Augustine's impromptu tour took Ben through the third floor, which included the employee gym and ping-pong stadium ("Competition's intense in this room," Augustine observed solemnly), and the fourth, which housed the employee kitchen ("A lot of creativity happens here") and the nursery/day-care center.

"Hiya, Amy!" he called out as they strode through the big day-care space on their way back to the elevator. His wave was returned wordlessly by an enormously pregnant woman who sat in a large chair reading a book to the collection of spellbound children gathered around her.

"People seem to love this place," commented Ben as they headed for the fifth floor.

"Our people *are* this place," Augustine replied. "Most folks think that Allen & Augustine builds chairs," he added, "and I suppose that's true. But what we really build is people."

By this time they had been through three floors, and Ben decided to ask the question that had been nagging in the back of his mind.

"So where exactly *is* your office?"

Augustine laughed. "Well, now, that's a good question. I guess you could say, you're walking through it."

Ben looked puzzled.

"I don't really have an office, per se. I spend my time pretty much up and down and all over these six floors."

As he spoke, they approached a scatter of desks, stools, tables, and upright panels all festooned with dozens of maps with large green areas drawn on and covered with pushpins.

"No *office*, per se?" The woman speaking sat at the center of this command post and was just hanging up a phone with a slightly beleaguered expression. "He doesn't have a *home*, per se! I swear, the man sleeps here."

Augustine shrugged and gave an embarrassed grin. "Only sometimes."

"Hi, you've gotta be Ben." The woman stuck out her hand. "I'm Annie." She looked at Augustine. "And I quit." Her deadpan was so perfect that Ben held his breath—until he realized from Augustine's grin that Annie was pulling his leg.

"Yeah, yeah," Augustine nodded. "I'll call Personnel. So how's it coming?"

At that moment another phone on her desk rang. "Hang on a sec." She picked up the phone and said, "Yah?" She shot a weary look at Augustine and slowly shook her head as she listened. "Okay," she sighed into the phone. "Well, let me know." Then, to Augustine: "Not so good. I'm working on a possible lead—but we haven't been able to reach him yet."

As Annie turned to speak with another employee, Augustine explained the situation to Ben.

A shipment of an exotic hardwood, which they needed to complete a major custom order, had been turned away from port on entry because of some import-regulation technicality ("Politics!" Augustine snorted) and was now back on a steamer bound for Asia, where it had originated.

"If we don't fulfill that order," Annie chimed in, "it will *really* hurt us."

"I know you're on it, Annie," said Augustine.

As he and Ben turned and began heading back toward the elevator, he added, "I don't know if this problem can be solved or not, but I'll tell you this—if anyone can find a way, it's Annie. She's the most resourceful person I've ever met."

From the corner of his eye Ben glimpsed a brief smile slip across Annie's face as she turned and picked up her phone again. Obviously, she'd overheard the remark. He suspected that had been intentional on Augustine's part.

"One more reason we vastly prefer to work with all domestic stock," Augustine was saying as they headed for the elevator. "But these days, we can't afford to be choosy. What the customer wants, the customer gets."

Just then they heard a loud cheer followed by a burst of applause from a huddle of employees gathered around Annie's desk.

Augustine stopped and watched them, beaming. "Unless I miss my guess, Annie just came through again."

Sure enough, they learned when they walked back to the scene, Annie's lead had finally come through: she had managed to track down a high-end home builder a few states away who'd had a mansion-upgrade project cancel on him and was looking to unload his stock of specialty lumber—including exactly the rare wood Augustine needed.

"We're saved," said Augustine. After a few moments of walking in silence, he added, "For today, anyway."

Ben instantly recognized this as a perfect moment to press his advantage and make his pitch. Augustine knew as well as Ben did how financially hemmed in they were.

That was, after all, why he was here.

But as he opened his mouth to make his play, he had a sudden image of Aunt Elle saying, "*Pull.* Not *push.*"

He closed his mouth again.

As they entered the elevator to head up to the next floor, he said, "So . . . Annie. Wow. She's a gold mine. Where'd you find her?"

Augustine chuckled.

"When Annie first showed up here, she was a single mom with two kids to feed. Never finished college, zero skills to speak of." He shook his head, marveling. "But she had one thing you couldn't miss: *empathy.* She could listen to people, and they'd feel *heard.* Know what I mean?"

Ben did know exactly what he meant. Melanie was like that. When Ben talked, Mel not only listened carefully to every word, it felt as though she listened *through* the words. She seemed to get what he was saying, even when he didn't feel he was doing a very good job saying it.

"So," Augustine continued, "we put her on the phones. And she was great. Everyone loved her. A few years later, we really needed someone to run Sourcing. So I offered it to her."

"Wait—to run the department?! I thought she had no skills. *Zero,* you said. What happened?"

Arriving at the sixth floor, Augustine stepped out and turned to look at Ben, pondering his question.

"What happened. Well . . . I guess I saw something in her that she didn't see in herself. You know what Winston Churchill had to say about this? He said: 'I have found that the best way to get another to acquire a virtue is to impute it to him.' Or to *her*, in this case."

Augustine shook his head and laughed.

"I just *love* that. Give people something good to live up to—something *great*—and they usually will. In fact, often they'll even exceed those expectations."

Noting the look of skepticism that flashed across Ben's face, Augustine boomed another big laugh, then took Ben by the arm and said, "Look here, for a moment."

He turned and sat down on one of the broad hardwood benches that lined the wall, ushering Ben to sit with him.

"You know about our colors?"

In fact, Ben had noticed this but hadn't given it any thought: the bench seat was shot through with threads and ribbons of brilliant color, a palette of oranges and reds, tans and yellows that reminded him of Vermont fall foliage. It was gorgeous.

"New England in October!" he commented. Suddenly he was curious. "So, how exactly do you get those colors? That isn't paint—is it some kind of dye?"

Augustine grinned.

"Nope. None of our woods are dyed, stained, or—heaven forbid!—painted. No solvents, no chemicals. We apply a clear varnish to protect it; that's it. But the coloring, that's our secret patented process. You'll never guess where those colors come from."

Ben shook his head.

Augustine ran his hand along the polished plank.

"Allen tell you about the big fire?"

Ben nodded. "Incredible. You lost everything."

Augustine looked thoughtful. "In a way. Lost, and found."

He thought for a moment, then went on, speaking quietly, almost as if talking to himself.

"Isn't that how it always is? Just when you think you've lost something so precious, you can't ever recover from it . . . and then, if you keep your eyes and heart open, you find that the loss has made room for something else of great value, something you would never have found otherwise?"

In fact, Ben did know what it was like to lose something precious—and he sure didn't see how that could lead to anything good. He also wasn't sure whether Augustine's musings invited a reply or not. After a moment he said, "So you're saying that fire somehow turned out to be a *positive*?"

Augustine smiled. "While we were poking through the charred mess the next day, we noticed something. A few of the larger, rough-cut maple planks hadn't burned, but they had been steeped in an intense steam when the fire department's spray first hit the place.

"They had not burst into flame—but they had burst into *color*."

They had started experimenting, he explained, and in time had come up with a method of heating the raw, untreated hardwood planks that brought out the natural sugars in the wood.

"Sort of like caramelizing," Augustine said. "We cook the wood, you could say."

Done correctly, the process brought out a whole palette of natural hues and shades within the wood itself. Using a variety of woods and varying the heat and "cooking" time with each, they had developed an amazing array of natural colors.

"So where do those incredible colors come from?" said Augustine. "*From inside the wood itself.* They were there all the time."

He cocked his head in the direction of Annie's station.

"Something like Annie. People have all sorts of amazing qualities and natural abilities trapped inside them. With the wood, it's knowing how to apply heat. With people, it's applying your belief."

He looked at Ben. "The other day, you described us as one of the city's great success stories. *That's* the key to our success, right there. Strategies and plans, projections and road maps—they don't make things *move*, they don't make things *happen*. If you're going to get anything done, you have to engage people."

He placed his hand on his chest and patted his heart a few times.

"And that starts here."

Ben nodded as he saw his moment. Preliminaries were over; it was time to engage.

"Well, that segues pretty well into the reason I'm here. Is it okay if we talk about the current situation for a moment?"

"Of course," said Augustine.

Ben ran his hand along the smooth plank, just as Augustine had done, marveling at the colors.

"It would be obvious to any observer," he said, "that your people are doing an incredible job. *But* . . . it's also obvious that they're fighting an uphill battle. Honestly, I think a *yes* vote Monday would open up a whole new chapter for Allen & Augustine . . ." and he proceeded to lay out his case for the merger.

Augustine listened, nodding, and didn't say a word until Ben was finished. Then he nodded one more time, slowly, and put his hand on Ben's shoulder.

"When we started, there were just the two of us, Allen and me, and a few friends, working out of that abandoned church. You saw our first chair, upstairs?"

Ben nodded.

"Did you know that was made out of wood from one of the church's front pews? Those first few dozen chairs we made by pulling apart our own office." He chuckled, shaking his head. "And then the fire finished the job for us. Amazing."

He stood up and pressed the elevator's DOWN button. Ben had the sense their tour was over.

"As I said," Augustine continued, "we were just a handful back then. And today we're five hundred people. Five *hundred*. I've never fired a single employee. The terms *layoff* and *cutback* are not in our vocabulary—and we're not about to start now.

"I like you, Ben, but I'm not naive. If you guys buy us, you and I both know what happens next. I lose half my people, like so many spare parts. Maybe more than half. And I'm not going to stand by and let that happen."

Ben started to protest, but Augustine held up his hand to stop him.

"Look, you've got your job to do, and I respect that. I have mine. And my job?—"

He nodded toward the halls and airy open office spaces of the sixth floor, where dozens of Allen & Augustine employees sat talking on phones to users of their fine chairs all over the country.

"—Is *their* jobs."

6

THE LANGUAGE
OF STRENGTH

When Ben was directed by Sal the maître d' toward what he now thought of as "their" table, he saw that, sure enough, both women were already there.

Ben was a roil of conflicting thoughts and emotions. On the one hand, he was very curious to learn more about Aunt Elle's history and business experience. (Had she made millions in the stock market? Been a super-successful real estate speculator?) At the same time, he was also struggling to sort through everything Augustine had said during their visit. And he was stinging from what felt like a total failure to advance the cause of his *yes* vote next Monday.

And so he did not notice at all when, as he strode across the room to join Claire and Aunt Elle, a stocky man at a nearby table suddenly pushed back his chair to get up from his seat, coffee in hand, and slid directly into Ben's path.

The two men collided perfectly, as if they had rehearsed it, sending the husky fellow back down into his seat and his coffee spilling out across the tablecloth—and down his jacket sleeve.

"Hey!" the big man barked as he lunged back to his feet, "whyntcha watch where you're goin'!"

"Me?!" Ben blurted out, "I was just minding my own—" but the big man went off on him, berating him for his clumsiness and demanding loudly to speak with the manager about his ruined suit. Ben felt blood rush to his face and was gearing up to defend himself when suddenly—

"Excuse me."

The tirade abruptly stopped, and Ben was startled to see Aunt Elle standing directly in front of the man, extending a moistened cloth napkin. How on earth had she gotten there so quickly?

"I'm so sorry," she said quietly, "this may be entirely my fault. I believe I distracted him. May I offer to pay for your dry cleaning?"

The big man worked his jaw once or twice, like a fish on dry land. Finally he took the proffered napkin and began wiping his sleeve.

"Naw," he managed, "it's . . . it's actually not that bad."

It was true: only a small bit of the coffee had actually gotten onto the sleeve, and it would easily come out with one good cleaning.

The man left the restaurant—after apologizing gruffly to Ben and (less gruffly) to Aunt Elle—and Ben accompanied Aunt Elle back to the table, where Claire awaited them with an amused look.

"Thank you!" he said to Aunt Elle once they were seated. "You saved my rear end—I thought he was about to knock me back into last week!"

"He reacted," said Aunt Elle. "I responded. There's a world of difference."

"I'll say," agreed Claire.

"Nothing ruins a good negotiation," Aunt Elle continued, settling herself into her seat and smoothing her napkin over her lap, "like one of the participants reacting. If more people responded instead of reacting, the world would be . . ."

Aunt Elle suddenly became aware that Ben was sitting still, studying her.

"Yes?" she said.

Ben stifled a smile. "You *yielded.*"

"I beg your pardon?" said Aunt Elle.

"You said, *The more you yield, the more power you have.* That's how you stopped that guy from ranting at me. You yielded."

Aunt Elle looked at Ben for a moment, then turned to Claire. "You see, he *does* listen. At least, every so often. It's a promising trait."

Ben felt a bit of heat flushing his cheeks—and then caught the slight crinkling at the corners of Aunt Elle's eyes and mouth.

He sighed. "I'm *reacting.*"

Claire burst out laughing.

Aunt Elle inclined her head an inch in his direction. "I was *having you on,*" she said with a demure smile. "*Yanking your chain*, as I believe you kids say these days.

"But you do, you know," she added. "*Listen*, I mean."

"Thank you," he replied. "And you lie."

Claire nearly choked on her salad.

"I beg your pardon?" said Aunt Elle again.

"Well," said Ben, "you told that guy that you believed you'd distracted me. You didn't distract me, and you knew it."

"Oh, that." Aunt Elle waved one hand vaguely. "Well, I *could* have. Anyway, you know what Aristotle said: 'It is the mark of an educated mind to rest satisfied with the degree of precision which the nature of the subject admits, and not to seek exactness where only an approximation is possible.'"

"Of course," said Ben with as straight a face as he could manage. "I was just saying exactly that to my wife the other day."

Aunt Elle arched one eyebrow.

Just then the waiter came to take their order. It was the same young man who had cleaned up the spilled coffee and dealt with the irate customer. When Ben apologized, he politely brushed it off—"*Niente*"—but it was plain to see that he was stressed. The place was *packed* today.

"Speaking of exactness, I've been thinking about what you said," Ben commented. "And I'm having a hard time seeing how it would actually apply. I mean, in real life. It seems to me, *yielding* means giving up any advantage you might have. Giving in, saying, *I give up, you win*, without even a fight."

Aunt Elle thought for a moment.

"May I ask," she said, "how did your meeting go today?"

Ben sighed. "Not that well. I got a tour, met a lot of people, gave it my best shot—and got shot down."

Aunt Elle nodded. "When you go into these meetings, do you ever think of it as 'engaging the enemy'? Suiting up to go into battle, like knights of old?"

Ben had to admit: this was exactly how he thought of it.

"Here," said Aunt Elle, and she held up one hand in front of her, palm toward Ben. "Put up your hand."

Ben did as he was told, and Aunt Elle pressed her hand against his. She was surprisingly strong, and it took some effort to resist her push.

"There," said Aunt Elle as she put her hand down again.

"Okay . . ." Ben waited for an explanation.

"When I pushed," she said, "why did you push back?"

Ben was startled to realize that he didn't really have an answer to that. "I don't know . . . I just did."

"And how did our hands *move* together?"

"Move together? They didn't budge."

Aunt Elle nodded. "Exactly. Would you call that a successful negotiation?"

Ben frowned. "So what are you saying would be the right way to go? When the other guy pushes, just give up?"

Aunt Elle pursed her lips. "Yielding *is* giving—but not giving *up*. Two very different things. I'll give you an example.

"Abraham Lincoln was once told by a reporter that another government official had sharply criticized him. What did the president have to say about that? 'I have great respect for the man,' replied Lincoln, 'and if he has concerns about me, there must be some truth to it.'

"The criticism was intended to draw Lincoln into a skirmish that would have distracted him from other business. Instead, his comment not only deflected the critique but also won the hearts of both friends and foes—and allowed the president to keep his focus on the more important issues at hand.

"Lincoln's maneuver," concluded Aunt Elle, "was what a boxer calls a *parry*."

"A boxer," repeated Ben, trying unsuccessfully to imagine Aunt Elle ringside at a boxing match.

"My son was a reasonably good boxer in his day," she explained.

"Watch a boxing match and you'll notice that when one fighter throws a jab—a straight punch, usually with the left hand," Aunt Elle demonstrated as she spoke, jutting her left hand out straight— "the target will wait until the punch almost hits him and then deflect it away with the slightest flick of the right wrist. And here's the amazing thing: the harder the punch, the less effort it takes to parry it.

"This is exactly what Lincoln did.

"So you see, it *is* about saying 'You win,'" said Aunt Elle, "but *You win* doesn't have to mean *I lose*. Quite the contrary. Letting the other person win is the beginning of one's own triumph."

Ben thought for a long moment, then slowly shook his head.

"I . . . sort of get what you're saying. But I'm not convinced."

Claire laughed.

Ben looked at her darkly. "Did I say something funny?"

"Uh-huh," she said. "You said Aunt Elle hasn't *punched* and *beaten* you yet."

Ben looked back helplessly at Aunt Elle. "I said that?!"

Aunt Elle was clearly amused. "*Convince* means *to overcome by argument*," she explained. "It comes from the Latin word for *conquer*. You know the expression: *A man convinced against his will . . .*"

". . . *is of the same opinion still*," said Ben.

"Exactly. And is there really any other way to be convinced—conquered, overcome by argument—than against your will?

"In other words, you're right: yielding *does* mean giving your power away. But the more you give away, the more you have."

Ben audibly groaned. "I'm sorry, I just don't get that. That sounds like a complete contradiction. It still seems to me, you give power away and people will walk all over you."

Aunt Elle looked at him disapprovingly and made a noise that sounded like "*Hmp*."

The waiter came with their meals, and they began to eat.

"How is your fish?" asked Aunt Elle.

To Ben's taste, it was actually a little dry, but he just nodded and said, "Good."

"Really." Aunt Elle's eyes narrowed. "I think it's *off*." She turned toward the kitchen with an upraised forefinger and called out, "*Scusi*, Marco?"

Ben was mortified. She was going to upbraid this poor waiter, who was already stretched to the breaking point, and send her food back?!

The harried young waiter was instantly back at tableside. "*Signora?*"

"Marco, who is cooking today?"

"Ah, Benedetto, *signora*."

"Wonderful." She set her napkin down and turned to face Marco directly. "I wonder if you would tell Benedetto that the sauce is absolutely exquisite. He has outdone himself."

Marco beamed and nodded. "*Certe, signora*."

"And . . ." Aunt Elle lifted her hand with that same upraised index finger. "I don't really know a great deal about this particular style—*trota alla griglia*, is it?" Marco bowed in the affirmative. "So I would definitely want to defer to Benedetto . . ."

Marco leaned forward, eyes intently on Aunt Elle to make sure he caught her every exact word. "*Si . . . ?*"

"I'm wondering if it's possible to prepare it just a bit less well done. That is, a little more on the *moist* side. If it isn't, I'll completely understand. But if it is, I would so appreciate it."

"*Assolutamente, signora! Subito!*"

Marco was already headed for the kitchen when Aunt Elle added, "Oh, and Marco?"

"*Si?*"

"Please tell Benedetto I adore the food here, and it gives me great pleasure to pay for it. I will be very cross if this dish is taken off my bill."

Marco smiled and bowed, then headed off to the kitchen. Aunt Elle turned to Ben and said, "So?"

Ben looked at her, confused. "So . . . ?"

"So what did you observe?"

It took Ben a moment. "Ohh," he said, the light gradually dawning. She had done all that on *purpose*; she was making a *point*.

"You weren't listening," she said crossly.

"No, no!" Ben protested. "I *was*. Okay, hang on." He thought for a second, then said, "You started out by complimenting the sauce."

"Everyone likes being acknowledged for doing a good job," she agreed. "And?"

"And you were obviously very polite." He thought another moment, then added, "You *responded* instead of *reacting*." He paused in thought once more and then said, "Come to think of it, so did he."

"*Excellent* observation." Aunt Elle practically beamed. "If I had reacted, chances are good Marco would have done likewise. Whether you react or you respond, it tends to foster the same behavior in the other person.

"Expecting someone to be helpful doesn't change *them*. It changes *you*. And that," she added with the faint trace of a smile, "is what changes *them*.

"Also, instead of insisting on being right, I gave *being right* to the chef. I let our waiter know what would make me happy, but that if they couldn't accommodate my request exactly as I'd asked, I wouldn't make a problem out of it."

"So . . . you gave away all your power," observed Ben.

"And did he walk all over me?" said Aunt Elle.

Ben held up his hands in a *You win* gesture.

Aunt Elle inclined her head. "You're welcome."

"Aunt Elle has a word for that," said Claire. And then she said in a stage whisper, as if pretending Aunt Elle couldn't hear her, "Are we surprised?"

Ben looked at Aunt Elle.

She nodded. "Yes. That would be an example of *tact*."

Tact?! Ben had to stop himself from laughing out loud. He was starting to think that Aunt Elle was one of the bluntest people he'd ever met.

Aunt Elle must have caught something in his expression, because she smiled slightly. "Oh, I know," she said. "I can be blunt. But *blunt* isn't the same thing as *tactless*. Sometimes directness is called for. But thoughtlessness? Never.

"Tact is not the same thing as compromise. Tact, in fact, is the *language of strength*."

Ben thought about that for a moment. "I hate to be dense," he began, "but how exactly is tact the language of strength? To me it seems like, I don't know . . ."

"The language of a weakling?" Aunt Elle gave another of her Sphinx smiles, a smile so slight you'd miss it if you blinked. "Well, let's look at it.

"*Tactful* and *tactile* both come from the same Latin word, which is the word for *touch*. Having tact literally means being *in touch* with the other person. And when you treat someone with tact, it allows them to stay *intact*.

"This goes back to the matter of influence," she added. "Ultimately, how effective you are, how *influential* you are, comes down to your intention. What are you focused on? *Your* benefit, or *theirs*?

"You've probably seen those talks, the ones where the speaker gets everyone all worked up to a fever pitch with an emotional story and then rallies them like drunken sports fans around some corporate mission . . ."

Ben had to admit, he had heard that speech.

He had *given* that speech.

"But getting people to do what you want them to, whether or not they really want it for themselves," Aunt Elle continued, "that's just manipulation. Any second-rate television commercial can do that."

Ben nearly winced. The day before, when Aunt Elle had asked him for a definition of *influence*, that was exactly what he had replied: *your ability to get people to do what you want them to.* And he knew Aunt Elle well enough by now to know that *she* would have remembered that, too.

"Now," she was saying, "getting people to do what *they* truly want? That's an achievement. As a good friend of mine says, *Your influence is determined by how abundantly you place other people's interests first.*"

"That sounds like Pindar," commented Claire.

Aunt Elle nodded and said, "Most influential person I've ever met."

"Wait," said Ben, "you know *Pindar*? The Chairman?!"

He felt his pulse race. The man known simply as the Chairman was something of a business legend. He was one of the most influential and successful businessmen and corporate consultants in the world.

"Of course," said Aunt Elle. "That's how I met Claire."

This was just too much. Ben pushed his chair back and threw his napkin down on the table in a gesture of exasperation.

"*You* know Pindar?!" he said to Claire. "And you didn't tell me?"

Claire laughed. "Not exactly. I mean, I've never actually met him in person. Let's say, we have a mutual friend." Noting Ben's flabbergasted expression, she added, "I'll tell you more about it—some other time. Promise."

"I can't believe you two are saying this," said Ben. "This is one of my biggest dreams. I have always wanted to meet the Chairman."

At that moment Marco returned with their fresh entrees, cooked to perfection—and with a personal note of thanks from Benedetto.

That night Ben again took out the book Melanie had given him, set it on the little desk, and gazed at it:

Ben's Manifesto

He sat, thinking about Aunt Elle's question again.

What *did* he really have to offer them? He was feeling less and less certain that he knew the answer. Staring at the book's cover, he gestured at it like a stage magician and muttered, "*Presto manifesto!*" and then sighed. It would be nice if the little volume's pages would magically reveal the answer.

Unlikely, though—considering it was mostly blank inside.

What was it Augustine had said? "How's our corporate raider doing this morning?" Is that what he was? A corporate raider?

He opened the book and looked at what he had written the night before on the first page:

Ben's Keys to Legendary Leadership

KEY #1: HOLD THE VISION

and now added another line to his list:

KEY #2: BUILD YOUR PEOPLE

Turning to another fresh page, he began to write down some thoughts from his day:

BUILD YOUR PEOPLE

Lead from the heart.

The more you yield, the more power you have.

The substance of influence is pull ... not push.

Tact is the language of strength.

Give people something good to live up to—
something great—and they usually will.

He thought for another moment, then added at the bottom:

And don't react—respond.

Ben felt Mel's presence even before he heard her slippered foot-falls. A moment later he felt her hands on his shoulders.

"Hi," she said.

"Hi," he said back.

"Whatcha doin'?"

He held the book up so she could see. Peering over his shoulder, she read what he'd been writing.

"So, those your car keys you got there?" she said.

He put the book down, stood up, turned around, and kissed her. "Nobody likes a wise guy," he said.

She smiled, then hugged him, leaned in close, and whispered in his ear, "Don't worry. We'll be okay."

7

THE WORK

Thursday Ben had arranged to spend his morning on the ground floor with Frank, VP of Production. When he arrived at the reception desk on the dot of nine, the burly man with tree-trunk hands was there waiting for him.

"I appreciate your taking the time to—" but before Ben could finish the sentence, Frank had thrust an apron and a set of heavy gloves into his hands.

"C'mon. Show you around."

Donning the gear as he walked, Ben followed Frank out to a row of loading docks in the back of the building, where several large trucks were unloading great stacks of lumber.

"Excellent," said Ben companionably. "I love a little workout."

Frank just grunted in reply. Ben suspected that Frank was not a man of many words.

As it turned out, it was a bit more than the "little workout" Ben was expecting. Two and a half hours later, as they hand-trucked the last load of wood to its station on the big open-span expanse of the production floor, Ben was flat-out exhausted.

Just as he was sitting down to rest, Frank beckoned him back to his feet—"You gotta see this"—and set off at a solid stride, with Ben scurrying to catch up. A minute later they were standing before a vast brick kiln lined with a sophisticated, computer-programmable sequence of steam jets. Ben was about to see how they *cooked the wood*.

The process was fascinating, and Ben watched, entranced, for another twenty minutes before they set off for Frank's office, Ben doing his best not to limp visibly.

On the way, Frank stopped to check in on a new employee who was busy hand-carving some intricate detail into the back of a large oak chair.

"Custom job," commented Frank. "Traditional all-wood joinery—mortise and tenon, no screws or nails, all pegs and shims."

Ben believed this was the longest sentence he had heard Frank speak all morning.

"Show you something?" Frank said to the young man as he took the tool from his hand. He sat and began carving out a scroll design in long, continuous, curving motions as his student observed carefully.

It was striking to see Frank's big hamlike fist curled around the tiny instrument, performing this delicate operation. Oddly graceful, thought Ben—like a lumberjack doing needlework.

"See?" said Frank, handing the tool back.

The young man nodded. "Thanks, Frank."

Frank grunted, "Good," and he and Ben were off again, walking the workroom floor.

"Taught the kid's dad," Frank said as they walked. "He'll be okay." He gave Ben a sideways glance as they walked. "You said you like to work out. Seen our gym?"

"Yes," Ben said. "It's a great idea. I'll bet you guys love having it right here in the building."

"Yeah, I keep meaning to go," said Frank. "But who's got time? Anyway, I get my workout right here."

Ben thought about that. "How long have you worked here, Frank?"

Frank barked a laugh. "How long? Forever."

They arrived at Frank's office, which was scarcely more than a desk and several chairs stuck in a twelve-by-twelve space at the far end of the production floor.

"Let's sit," said Frank, an offer Ben gratefully and immediately accepted. "Coffee?" Ben accepted this offer eagerly, too. Frank took a bottle of water.

"So, you've seen the brothers?"

Ben nodded. "Augustine yesterday, Allen Tuesday."

"Right." Frank shook his head and coughed out another laugh. "Without vision the people perish, blah blah blah. I've heard it. Tell you what, they'll perish a whole lot faster without *food*."

He took a long slug of water.

"Don't get me wrong. I love those guys. I'd follow them over a cliff." (Ben thought this was a telling choice of images—he was afraid Frank and the rest of the company might be on the verge of doing exactly that.) "But . . . well, can I be frank?"

"Of course—" Ben started to say, when Frank exploded with a loud guffaw.

"Sorry," Frank said. "Dumb joke. 'Can I be Frank?' What else could I be?" He let out one more guffaw, then grew instantly serious again.

"Tell you what. Allen's got his head in the clouds half the time. And Augustine? Guy's got a heart of gold, which is great, but if you ask me, he can go a little overboard sometimes on the whole touchy-feely thing."

"Frank?" One of Frank's crew poked his head in the door of Frank's office. He looked worried.

"Yeah," Frank shot back. "Hang on."

He turned back to Ben and said, "But I'll tell you one thing about those two nobody can argue. They know every inch of this business. They've paid their dues."

Turning back to the man at the door, he said, "Shoot."

"That order Annie placed? Those construction guys, with the Asian hardwood? We gotta get a truck out there today, but nobody can tell us how much the stuff weighs, so we don't know if a two-ton rig will do, or if we need a ten-ton. And they're not answering their phones."

Frank's brow furrowed in thought.

"The project budget won't let us send the bigger truck unless we absolutely need it," the man added. "But if the two-ton turns out to be too small, we'll lose the whole order."

Frank nodded and said, "Send the two-ton. It'll work."

"Right." The man disappeared from view.

"How can you make a decision like that," Ben wondered aloud, "when you don't have enough information to know whether you're right or not?"

"That's why they call it a *decision*," replied Frank. "If you had all the information, there'd be nothing to it. But sometimes you have to decide, even when you don't have all the information.

"Besides," he added, "I'm pretty sure I'm right."

"Really." Ben was skeptical. "How so?"

Frank looked at Ben. "I know wood."

Ben thought Frank's comment about making decisions left an

opening big enough for a twenty-ton truck to drive through. And the morning was nearly gone. Time to bring it home.

"Well, you guys sure have a big decision to make Monday."

Frank nodded.

"And I want to make sure I give you as much good information as I can, so you can make the best choice possible. For you and for your crew."

Frank nodded again. "Okay."

In a few sentences, Ben laid out his case for how and why a marriage with the Marden Group would be the right move for Allen & Augustine. When he was finished, he looked at Frank.

Frank took a few more swigs from his water bottle, nearly draining it, then looked at Ben.

"Ben," he said, "let me be—"

"Frank?" offered Ben.

The big man's face relaxed a bit as he laughed. "Yeah, that too. I was going to say, let me be blunt."

He pointed upward at the floors above them.

"I told you I'd follow Allen and Augustine anywhere. And I would. These guys?" He jerked a thumb in the direction of the crew out on the production floor.

"I dunno if they'd go over a cliff for the brothers, but I'll tell you what, they'd follow *me* anywhere. Why? One reason: they respect me. Why? Because I know my pegs and shims.

"You can't run a tight operation unless your people trust you. Not the boardroom, not the market research. You. And they won't—not unless you trust yourself." Frank gave himself a hearty *smack!* of his fist against his substantial gut. "Right here."

Ben hesitated. He recalled only too well that disastrous straw poll he had invited in the boardroom a few days earlier. But the question had to be asked.

"So," he said, "what is your gut saying right now about the vote on Monday?"

Frank's expression was hard to read, but Ben was pretty sure he knew what it said: *Why should I trust you?*

Frank drained his water bottle and tossed it across the room into a trash can on the other side of the little office—a perfect basket—then turned back to Ben.

"It hasn't decided yet."

8

BEING MUDDY

"No Aunt Elle?" When Sal ushered him to the familiar corner table, Ben had found Claire sitting alone with a basket of breadsticks.

"She asked me to convey her regrets. She couldn't make it today."

Ben felt a stab of disappointment. He'd been looking forward to more conversation with Aunt Elle.

On the other hand, now he could talk more freely with Claire about his situation. And that was the whole point, he reminded himself. *Intel. The inside scoop.* Right? This was a golden opportunity.

"So," said Claire as Ben settled into his seat and picked out a meal from the menu, "how's Mel doing?"

The three of them had first met and become friends in business school. Twelve years ago, when Ben and Melanie went through a rough patch together, it was Claire who had helped pull them through. That was all in the past now, and their life was good . . . except that Mel had lost her job six months ago, and all her efforts at finding a new one had so far proven fruitless.

Which meant it was all the more critical that Ben bring this merger to a successful conclusion.

"She's good," replied Ben. "Great, actually. She loves being an at-home mom for a change. And Robbie sure isn't complaining any."

He went on to brag about Robbie for a few minutes—at age eleven, he was already an accomplished martial artist, had just passed his black-belt test ("with *honors*," Ben added), and was doing great in his schoolwork, too.

"But hey," Ben said, "before we get into anything else, you promised me you'd tell me about Pindar. And Aunt Elle—who exactly *is* she, anyway? And what kind of work did she do?"

Marco, the young waiter, came by to take their lunch order, and after he left, Claire addressed Ben's questions.

"That mutual friend I mentioned? It's Rachel, my boss.

"Before starting her own business, she used to work for Pindar and his wife at their mansion. That's how she met Aunt Elle. There was a whole circle of prominent businesspeople who used to pass through Pindar's home, and Aunt Elle was one of them. I think Pindar had consulted for her company or something.

"Anyway, Rachel and Aunt Elle became thick as thieves. Today Aunt Elle is one of the biggest individual donors to Rachel's foundation."

Ben's mind was reeling. So Aunt Elle wasn't just wealthy, she was . . . *stratospherically* wealthy.

"What did Aunt Elle *do*? I mean, what was her business?"

Claire smiled. "She's a pretty private person, believe it or not. I'd have to let her tell you that. I'm sure she will sometime. She did tell me a story once, though, about how Pindar got started.

"As a young man, Pindar sold business machines. This was in the days before personal computers.

"He'd held a number of odd jobs, none of them especially successful, but at one point he made a conscious decision to excel. Now, as a freshman rep for this small firm, he paid a visit to a promising new company that was about to go through the roof—although of course nobody knew this yet.

"Pindar was not the only one trying to land this particular account. In fact, as it turned out, there were four other salesmen, from four other companies—including NCR, IBM, and a few other big names—all wooing the same client.

" 'They were all more skilled salespeople than I,' the Chairman told Aunt Elle. 'Every single one of them. They were all more experienced, and all far more accomplished—' "

"But—let me guess," said Ben. "He got the account?"

"He did. And when the company took off, so did Pindar's business. Soon he formed his own agency just to handle that account. More clients followed. And that was the first in what became a long line of successful ventures that built his fortune."

"So why was he the one who got the account?" asked Ben.

Claire laughed. "That's exactly what *I* said when I first heard the story. 'Well,' said Aunt Elle, 'those others may have known more about selling, but he knew *the machines*, inside and out, backwards and forwards, every feature and capability—every *jot and tittle*, as he put it.' "

"So he was really into business machines?" asked Ben.

"Not really. It wasn't about the machines—it was about the *client*. Pindar's gift is entrepreneurship, not electronics, and over the years he built businesses in many different fields. But whatever he did, he always took the time to make sure he understood what it was his clients needed, and *exactly* how his product or service would fulfill that need.

"When Pindar went in for that interview, there wasn't a question they asked that he couldn't answer. He was *prepared*.

"The client took this as a gesture of respect for them and their time—which was exactly what it was—and gave him the contract on the spot."

"And look what happened . . ." murmured Ben.

Claire nodded. "Corporations started paying him huge sums for his advice, because they knew that *he* knew what he was talking about. He'd done the work."

Marco brought their meals, which Claire greeted with enthusiasm.

"I'm starved," she said as she took the first bite. (The *trota alla griglia*, it was—this time done to perfection.)

"Aunt Elle says that's one of Pindar's success secrets that people often miss. Every field he's gone into, every business he's started, he's done at some point with his own hands, learning it nuts and bolts, from the ground up.

"Pindar himself says his number-one secret is *giving*. You heard Aunt Elle describe his Law of Influence: 'Your influence is determined by how abundantly you place other people's interests first.'

"Aunt Elle says that's all true . . . but that there's more to it. He's a very giving person—and he also knew how to *do the work*.

"Rachel asked Pindar once, with all those high-rolling CEOs coming through his home, with his incredible reputation and all the huge sums of money flowing through his hands, how did he keep all that from going to his head?

"He laughed and said, 'Yes, there's a lot of voltage flowing here. But it doesn't fry my circuits—because I stay grounded.'"

"*Grounded*," repeated Ben. "What do you suppose he meant by that?"

"That's exactly what I asked Rachel," replied Claire. "She thought for a moment, and then told me another Pindar story.

"At one of the Chairman's legendary parties, she met a wonderful older gentleman, a retired business leader named Le Herron. Le—he spells it *L-e* but pronounces it *Lee*—served for nearly two decades as CEO of OM Scott & Sons, now known as Scotts, the lawn-and-garden company.

"A few years after he took that position, the company's owners sold it to a big conglomerate. Many of the employees felt betrayed. It was up to Mr. Herron to make the transition work. And did he ever! Over the next ten years, the company's sales nearly tripled, its net income increased by 560 percent, and he took Scotts from being a good company to being a *great* one."

At Pindar's party that night, Claire explained, Herron had related an experience he had during World War II, as a brand-new second lieutenant in the Army Corps of Engineers.

He had been out with troops in the field on a training mission. It had been a hard day, and when the mess line was ready, he went over to eat—but before he could be served, an old sergeant took him aside.

"Lieutenant," said the sergeant, "*after* your men have been fed, if there's any food left, *then* you will eat. And later, *after* all your troops have been bedded down, if there's a place for you to lie down, *then* you will sleep."

"Wait." Ben couldn't stop himself from interrupting Claire's story. "A sergeant, correcting a *lieutenant*? Isn't that kind of, um, unusual?"

Claire laughed. "I'll say. That took chutzpah. But Le *listened* to him. 'In that moment,' he told the group at Pindar's, 'that sergeant taught me a leadership lesson that has formed the core of my beliefs ever since.'"

Claire laughed again, picturing the old sergeant putting the lieutenant in his place.

"Rachel said Pindar just *loved* that story," she added, "and he went around repeating it to everyone he knew who hadn't already heard it. He just loved the fact that this lieutenant was willing to learn from his sergeant.

"And *that*, says Rachel, is what keeps Pindar grounded, as far as she's concerned: his *humility*. 'If you want to be hugely successful,' she says, 'you have to stay hugely humble.'"

Ben gave a short laugh. "*Hugely humble.* Now *there's* an oxymoron."

Claire took another bite and looked at Ben thoughtfully. "Shall I tell you Aunt Elle's take on humility?"

"Please," said Ben. It struck him as fascinating that, even though Claire's mentor was not with them today, her presence somehow still seemed to command the conversation.

"Aunt Elle says there are few terms more misunderstood in our culture. People often equate humility with a lack of confidence or self-esteem, or think that being humble means being weak. 'And of course'"—here Claire lifted her chin and peered along her nose at Ben—"'they have it backwards. The more humble you are, the more personal power you have.'"

Ben had to laugh. Claire did a very credible Aunt Elle impression.

"She says the word *humility* shares a common root with *humus*. Being humble means being aware of your connection with the dust of the earth.

"The soil, she says, is the source of everything we have. 'Remember your muddy beginnings, and you can accomplish anything.'"

"That sounds like her," Ben commented. He hoped that Aunt

Elle's little saying might actually be true, because he certainly was feeling muddy right now. About everything.

"Here's another Elleism," continued Claire. " 'People who achieve great things that the world will never forget, start out by accomplishing small things that the world will never see.'

"Leaders don't expect anyone else to do anything they haven't done themselves. They get dirt under their nails and mud on their boots . . ."

Ben wasn't sure if this was Claire quoting Aunt Elle now, or Claire simply being Claire. Given all the time the two had spent in each other's company, perhaps this was a distinction without a difference.

"Abraham Lincoln *knew* law," Claire was saying. "He'd practiced it in freezing-cold, bare-floored small-town courtrooms. So did Gandhi. They both emancipated millions—but only because they knew the feel of the craft in their hands. George Washington knew the land. As a boy, Sam Walton milked the family cow and sold the surplus milk to neighbors. Bill Gates spent thousands of hours as a teenager programming computers.

"You know what Andrew Marden did? I mean, before he was the CEO of a vast conglomerate?"

"He was a merchant," Ben replied immediately, happy to have a question for which he *knew* that he knew the answer. "Sold dry goods, textiles, that kind of thing."

Claire laughed. "*Before* that. You should ask your boss sometime."

She stopped talking for a bit to work on her meal. Ben picked at the edges of his.

After a long minute of silence, Claire looked up and gave her old friend a level gaze.

"So, Ben. How's it going?"

Ben realized that, without quite meaning to, he'd been avoiding talking about his situation at Allen & Augustine. And wasn't that the very reason he was here with Claire in the first place? To try to gain the inside scoop?

He looked at his plate as he spoke. "Well, that merger I'm working on? It's . . . with someone you know. Someone you've worked with in the past."

Claire nodded. "Allen & Augustine."

He looked up sharply. "You already knew?!"

"I had a pretty good idea. So let me guess: you spent the morning today with Frank, walking the production floor?"

Ben squinted at Claire. How did she know so much? "Yeah. Why, does it show?"

She gave a little laugh. "I thought you looked a little shell-shocked. So you've already met with Augustine? And with Allen?"

Ben nodded. "And tomorrow, Karen."

"Ah," said Claire. "Well, she won't mince words."

Before Ben had a chance to ask what she meant by *that*, Claire reached over and poked him.

"Hey, trivia: you know who made the very first Allen & Augustine chair?"

All right! *This* one he knew, no question. "I sure do," he replied. "I sat in it myself on Tuesday. Nearly gave me a heart attack, too, when I realized I was sitting on a piece of company history. Allen made it."

Claire laughed again. "Nope. Allen had the idea—he *designed* the chair. But he didn't *build* it. That was Frank."

Frank! Ben whistled. He recalled asking Frank how long he'd worked at the company. What had Frank said? *Forever.*

"The last time I was there," Claire continued, "I remember thinking that big old brick building would fall down like an untied stack of kindling if Frank weren't down there on that first floor, holding it up."

They both chuckled for a moment at the picture that evoked, and then they fell silent again.

"So," Claire repeated gently, "how's it going?"

Ben sighed. "Claire, I think I'm in over my head. Mel and I really, *really* need this to happen. Bushnell obviously wants it badly, and I think my job is on the line. And heaven knows, Allen & Augustine certainly need it to happen, too. But I've met with three of the four levers of power there, and so far I'm oh-for-three."

He looked up at Claire.

"You have any brilliant ideas? Because I think I'm fresh out."

Claire took the last bite of her grilled trout and pondered the question.

"What does Mel say?"

Ben sighed again. "She says she believes in me."

"Well," said Claire, "she's pretty smart. Maybe you should follow her lead."

Ben took a distracted bite of a breadstick. Despite his workout that morning on Frank's loading dock, he wasn't very hungry. "Thanks, Yoda. So that's your brilliant idea?"

Claire set her fork down and looked at him.

"Ben, you don't have to be brilliant. The brilliant will take care of itself. You just need to *do the work*."

A sense of fatigue came over Ben, and suddenly he felt overwhelmed.

"You can't worry about the outcome," Claire added quietly.

"Just do the work. And not only because it needs doing, but also because that's the only way you'll generate real respect."

Ben nodded glumly.

Claire reached over and put her hand on his. "Ben, I'm not talking about gaining *their* respect. I'm talking about *your* respect. You want these people to trust you? Trust yourself.

"Listen, humility doesn't mean self-abasement, or devaluing your own worth. You can only be genuinely humble if you have enormous self-respect. *That's* something I learned from Pindar, even though I never met him—because it shines through the people he associates with, the people I *have* met.

"Self-respect is where every other kind of respect comes from. Respect from others is a reflection, not the source. It's not like, 'Oh, if my boss respected me, if my son respected me, if the world respected me, that would be great . . .' as if having respect from those other people would somehow generate your own respect for yourself.

"That'd be like asking the moon to make the sun shine. It doesn't work that way."

Ben was silent for a moment, then looked up at Claire and said, "You know, you're pretty Zen yourself."

"Ha," said Claire. "Thanks, Grasshopper."

As he walked back up the street toward the parking garage to fetch his car, Ben shook his head in disbelief. He'd just had an entire lunchtime alone with Claire—his "golden opportunity"—and he'd squandered it talking about himself.

"Way to go for that valuable *intel*," he muttered as he walked. "Keep your feet in the mud, stay connected to the humus. *That's* what you got for inside scoop?"

Still, despite his own mumbled complaints, he felt himself turning over in his mind the things Claire had said. Somewhere inside, they had touched a chord.

That night, Ben added one more key to his "manifesto":

KEY #3: DO THE WORK

On the next blank page, he carefully wrote down a few thoughts that had stayed in his mind from his morning at Allen & Augustine and his talk with Claire at lunch:

DO THE WORK

Lead from your gut.

Know your pegs and shims.

Stay hugely humble.

Stay grounded.

Get mud on your boots.

And trust yourself.

9

BIRTH AND DEATH

Friday morning at 9:05, Ben emerged from the old brick building and stood on the sidewalk outside, struggling to decide what to do.

When he had arrived at reception five minutes earlier to keep his appointment with Karen, the VP of Finance and Personnel, there was a message waiting for him, asking if he would meet her at the hospital. Ben's heart had leaped into his throat. The hospital?! Had something terrible happened?

Ben did not like hospitals.

It had been more than a decade since he had set foot in one, and it would be fine with him if it were ten more decades before he did so again. He honestly didn't know how he could go meet Karen there.

But how could he *not* go?

"Monday's board meeting is on the line here, Ben," he muttered, standing on the sunlit sidewalk. "Every vote counts." Especially one as influential as Karen's. He couldn't afford to blow off this appointment; he might not get another chance.

He headed up the street for the parking garage.

He found the petite woman with the intelligent dark eyes sitting on a bench just outside Emergency, smoking a cigarette.

"Glad to see you're okay!" he said. "What happened?"

"Amy, one of our customer service agents—"

"I met her," said Ben. "The enormously pregnant one."

Karen nodded slowly. "Enormously pregnant. That's Amy." She took a drag on her cigarette. "She's gone into labor, way ahead of schedule. Complications."

For the second time today, Ben's heart lurched. "Is the baby okay?"

Karen stubbed out the cigarette and got to her feet. "Actually, no." She grabbed a satchel from the ground by her feet and headed inside with Ben in tow, talking to him over her shoulder as they trod the halls.

"It started in the middle of the night. Both of them are in critical condition. The baby's in Neonatal, Amy's isolated in Critical Care."

They entered an elevator, and Karen punched 3.

Ben glanced at the elevator directory to see what was on the third floor. After a moment, he asked, "So . . . why are we going up to Oncology?"

"Another one of our employees, Phoebe in Accounting, has a grandmother here. She's not doing well. Doesn't get many visitors."

The elevator door opened and they walked down a series of hallways until they arrived at Phoebe-in-Accounting's grandmother's room, where they stopped and waited. A moment later a nurse emerged from the room and said, "They're doing a procedure now. She's sedated, but you can go in and sit in just a few minutes."

Ben and Karen took their seats on a small bench in the hall.

"Planning to be here long?" said Ben. He nodded at her satchel, which was overflowing with papers, files, and, Ben guessed, probably a small laptop. "Looks like you brought your whole office with you."

Karen patted the satchel. "Yup. It could be a while."

"Not to seem unfeeling," said Ben, "but if she's not even awake, and if Amy is in Critical Care and not taking visitors, then why are you here? I mean, there's nothing you can do."

"No," Karen replied. "But it's not about *doing*. It's about *being* here."

Ben thought about that.

"Anyway," she said, "you're here. So let's talk. You're here to talk about the merger."

"Right," said Ben.

"You saw Allen and Augustine?"

Ben nodded.

"And yesterday, probably, Frank?"

Ben nodded again.

Karen gave a little laugh. "The three musketeers."

"Is that what they call themselves?"

"It's what I call them—Management, Marketing, Manufacturing. All for one and one for all. I guess that makes me D'Artagnan."

She paused, and Ben suspected that if they were still outside, she would be taking another Bette Davis drag on a cigarette.

"Want some hospital coffee?"

"Sure," said Ben. They got up and walked slowly down the hall as they talked.

"They're good guys, the three musketeers," Karen said, "and they all see important aspects of the business. *Aspects*. But I sign every check. I know every name, every face. When business is down, I feel the impact it has on every single employee."

Arriving at the little alcove that served as a coffee station, Karen poured out two cups.

"Touch of half-and-half, one sugar," said Ben in answer to Karen's querying look. She took hers black.

"Finance and Personnel," Ben mused. "That's kind of a funny combination."

He took a sip of coffee. It was likely the worst coffee he'd ever tasted.

"Not really," said Karen. "Money is more than numbers on a ledger. Money is where it all gets real. Money is an organization's lifeblood.

"Monday you said you were here to help the bleeding stop. I deal with the bleeding every hour of every day."

She looked down into her coffee cup as if the answers to life's mysteries might be read there.

"Maybe," she mused, "a transfusion from your company *is* exactly what we need to survive . . ."

Ben quickly took another awful sip in an effort to mask any hint of reaction on his face—but inside, he was feeling a surge of jubilation. That sure sounded like a *yes* vote to him!

"And," she continued, "maybe it's not. Maybe we can survive the blood loss on our own."

Ben's jubilation faded.

"Look," Karen continued. "The economy's bad right now. Ten years ago it was great. Ten years from now? Who knows?"

She tasted her coffee, made a face, then took another sip.

"My point: Economies rise and fall. Circumstances change. We bleed. We heal. We grow. Sometimes we end up in Critical Care.

We can't control any of it, not really. What we *can* control is *who we are.*

"And bottom line, that's the only thing that counts."

Ben had no idea what to say, so he forced himself to have another slug of coffee.

Karen watched him, and then surprised him with an impish grin. "It's really deadly, isn't it?"

Ben laughed. "Truly."

Karen looked down into her coffee cup again, then back up at Ben.

"Why are you here, Ben? I mean, I know it's your job. But why are you here, *really?*"

"Wow," said Ben. "And I thought *Frank* was direct." He expected her to laugh, but she didn't, so he considered her question. "Bottom line?" he said. "I want to see Allen & Augustine recapture its former glory."

Karen looked at him for a moment. Then she said, "Do you believe in this company, Ben?"

"Absolutely!" he said without hesitation.

Karen looked faintly amused. "That's a strong word. So your belief in our company is *absolute?*"

Ben hesitated, and Karen continued.

"Let me ask you this: Would you lay down your life for this company?"

Now Ben was taken aback. "Whoa, I—" he began, but Karen cut him off.

"Don't worry, I don't think it'll exactly come to that." Again, that faint smile. "But here's my point. People use words awfully casually. They say, 'I'd give *anything* to . . .' Or, 'I'll bet *anything* that . . .' Really? *Anything?*"

She shook her head and took another swig of coffee. Ben had the idea that she would have been right at home throwing back a slug of rotgut rye at a stand-up bar in the Wild West.

As the sheriff.

"Well," she said, "you'll never hear me say, 'I would give my life for this company.' Or 'I would give my life for these people.'"

She looked at him.

"You know why you'll never hear me say that?"

Ben did not know.

"Because of the word *would*," said Karen. "It's not 'I *would* give my life for these people.' I *do* give my life for them. Every day. And they give it, too.

"That's why I'm here today. That's what we do. That's who we are."

She drained the paper coffee cup, crushed it, and tossed it in the trash.

"I honestly have no idea if this merger is a good idea, a great idea, or a terrible idea. Here's what I do know. You want my vote? You want me to encourage others to trust you with their vote?"

Her cell phone rang, and she glanced at the number as she kept talking.

"People will only trust someone when they know where he stands. Where do you stand, Ben? And what do you stand for?"

Before Ben could answer, she flipped open the phone and spoke into it. "Hang on." Then, to Ben: "I have to take this, outside. May be a while."

She left Ben there.

A moment later, another nurse emerged from the patient's room and called softly down the hall to Ben, "You can go in now." Before he could reply, she walked down the hall the other way and disappeared around a corner, leaving Ben alone outside the patient's room.

Ben felt torn. Should he stay and wait for Karen? Or just leave? He didn't really see the point in sticking around; he suspected they had said as much as they were going to say on the subject of the merger.

He looked at the door to the patient's room. *Doesn't get many visitors*, Karen had said. He took a deep breath, and let it out.

He opened the door and quietly stepped into the patient's room.

The woman was fast asleep, but her breathing was shallow and troubled. Slowly, uncertainly, he lowered himself into the chair by her bed.

Do the work, Claire had said. So . . . was this the work?

Ben didn't mind unloading tractor-trailers, or hauling pallets of lumber, or even sweeping warehouse floors. But sitting in a hospital room, the smells of medicine and bleach and illness all around him, sitting with someone he didn't even know and who almost certainly didn't know he was there? This was not something he'd signed up for. But here he was.

He reached over and took the woman's papery hand in his. She didn't stir.

There was no sound but the *tick-whirrrr, tick-whirrrr* of the machinery, giving the woman oxygen and monitoring her vital signs.

As he sat, holding Phoebe-in-Accounting's grandmother's hand, Ben replayed his conversation with Karen.

Where do you stand, Ben? And what do you stand for?

That was easy: God, family, country. And the Marden Group. Right? That's what he *supposed* he stood for. But at that moment, for some reason Ben couldn't identify, the words felt more like abstractions than a vivid personal truth.

Tick-whirrrr . . . tick-whirrrr . . .

What precisely *did* he stand for?

He didn't think he'd ever asked himself that question.

10

AN IMPRINT ON THE SOUL

Ben arrived at the busy café a good two hours later than he had on the previous days, sure that his lunch companions would be long gone. And indeed, as he approached the corner table, Claire was nowhere to be seen. Much to his surprise, though, Aunt Elle was there, having tea and, evidently, waiting for him.

"Claire said she is so sorry, but she couldn't wait any longer," said Aunt Elle.

Ben apologized for being so late, and explained briefly about his morning at the hospital, about the mother and child in Critical Care.

In fact, although he didn't go into these details with Aunt Elle, he had spent quite a while in the grandmother's room in Oncology, thinking. Finally he had left to go hunt Karen down, and had found her in the waiting room in Neonatal, where they sat together waiting for any news.

Ben hastily ordered a salad, and Aunt Elle ordered another pot of hot water for her tea. Just as the waiter turned to head back to the kitchen with their order, Ben had an afterthought and asked if he could also have a hot cup of coffee—fresh, *delicious* coffee—

right away. He was eager to get the sense memory of that hospital out of his nostrils and taste buds.

"How is your week going?" Aunt Elle inquired politely. "Your project?"

The waiter set a cup of hot coffee in front of Ben, and he sipped gratefully at the exquisite brew. He could hardly believe how good it tasted.

"Well . . ." He thought about how to answer her question. "The day we first met, you asked me, what did I have to offer them?"

Aunt Elle nodded.

"When the week began, I was pretty clear I knew the answer to that question. Now I'm not so sure."

She regarded him thoughtfully.

"Years ago," she said, "when I was in a position where I was often called upon to speak before large audiences, my father gave me some advice. 'Elle,' he said, 'never let 'em see you sweat. If people sense you're not in control, they'll eat you for lunch. When you get up there to give your talk, it's all right to be nervous—just don't let it show.'"

Aunt Elle laughed.

"Usually my father's advice was brilliant. In this instance, it was abysmal.

"I did what he said, or tried to, anyway. Just once. It was horrendous. Oh, I stood up there on the dais and put on a good show, pretending to be omniscient and invincible. My talk that afternoon, without question or doubt, stank to high heaven. Afterward I lay sick in bed for three days straight.

"It was awful."

Her delivery of the story was so dramatic that Ben could not help chuckling. "I'll bet you wish you had that on video."

She frowned. "And *that* would be a wager you would lose," she sniffed. Despite the frown, Ben could tell she was enjoying herself immensely.

"In any case," she continued, "I vowed never again to pretend to be someone I was not. And that was a vow I kept.

"The next time I spoke before a group, my nervousness was even greater—and I told them so. 'I just want you all to know, I am petrified' was my opening line. 'I hope you enjoy the next forty-five minutes. Myself, I'll be closing my eyes—let me know when it's over.'

"Everyone in the hall laughed. And you know, I could feel the audience rooting for me, reaching out to help me feel at ease. Instead of being merely the audience, they became my partners."

Ben laughed out loud. He could easily picture Aunt Elle as a younger woman, confessing to her audience and being buoyed by their collective empathy.

"The point I'm making, Ben, is this.

"Leadership is not something you can put on and take off, like a set of clothes. Your capacity to influence is not something you can rehearse, like a speech in a play.

"People, contrary to popular belief, are not fools. No matter what front you put on, they will read you, consciously or unconsciously—the *you* behind the words."

"Hang on," said Ben. "Are you saying it doesn't really matter what you say? That there's ultimately no point in choosing your words carefully? Because that sure doesn't sound like you."

"No, it doesn't." Aunt Elle smiled and took a sip of her hot tea. "And that's not what I'm saying.

"It's not that what you say isn't important. It is. That's just not where the source of your power lies." She took another sip as Ben tried to parse the logic of her statement.

"What you have to give," she continued, "you offer least of all through what you say; in greater part through what you do; but in greatest part through who you *are*."

Ben's salad came, and he suddenly realized how truly hungry he was.

As he began eating, Aunt Elle said, "How are the mother and child? Do we know?"

Ben nodded and swallowed a bite.

"They're okay. Actually, that's why I was so late getting here. I wanted to wait and find out if they were going to . . . you know, find out how they were doing."

"That could have taken hours," observed Aunt Elle.

"Yeah," Ben agreed between bites. "Actually, it did. A few, anyway."

Aunt Elle looked at Ben for a long moment before speaking again.

"Ben, may I ask you a personal question?" she said softly.

Ben laughed. "You've been doing nothing else all week. I don't see why we'd stop now."

Aunt Elle did not smile. "No, I mean *truly* personal."

Ben put his fork down. "Okay."

She paused, then said, "Have you . . . lost someone? Someone close to you?"

Ben sat back in his seat, thunderstruck. How did she know?

It had been more than a decade since it happened. An illness Ben could barely pronounce, let alone comprehend. It had been so unexpected—and so terribly swift. Less than a week, it had taken, for everything to go from normal to unthinkable.

It had been many long months before Ben and Melanie could even manage a conversation about the idea of having another child.

All at once, the house had grown still and quiet. The quiet remained for months, and then a year had gone by.

In time, bit by bit, sounds began to find their way back into Ben and Melanie's home. Then Robbie was born, and before long, almost without Ben realizing it was happening, the house was busy and full again. But there was a quiet inside of Ben that never left, and would never leave. And somehow, Aunt Elle had sensed this.

He looked at her with amazement.

"Yes." He nodded slowly. "We had a son." He thought for a moment, then added, "Oh. Claire must have told you."

She shook her head. "No. Claire is *very* good at respecting privacies."

"Then how . . . ?"

"It shows, dear," she said gently. "Life leaves a mark. None of us passes through the experience of our days unblemished or pristine. We all suffer tragedies and disappointments, struggles and failures. Losses great and small, and every one of them hurts.

"Life leaves a mark," she repeated.

Ben was quiet.

"We can try to cover it up, although if we do, we just tend to grow bitter on the inside. Or, we can embrace who we are—that is, who we are in the process of becoming. Embrace the hurt and it deepens you, makes you a richer person. Deny, reject, hold it at bay, fight it off, and it simply hardens you.

"Either way, it engraves itself onto your soul."

She paused to take another sip of hot tea, and to let the words sink in.

"So," she continued, "what do you have to offer those people? I'm not sure I know the answer, either.

"I know that competence counts. If you want people to follow you, they need to trust that you know what you're doing. But that's the smaller part of it. They need to trust your competence, yes, but even more, they need to trust your *character*.

"Competence is simply the baseline, the thing that puts you in the game. It matters, but honestly, it's a dime a dozen.

"Character, though. Character is that rare, precious gem, and anyone who possesses it is worth a great deal to the world around him.

"My father used to say, 'You can judge someone's character by what he does when no one's watching.' I believe *that* was one of my father's finer utterances."

She looked kindly at Ben.

"I suppose that prompts the question, What creates character? I think . . . perhaps it's the choices you make. How you choose to respond to what life throws at you."

Ben was still unable to speak. Aunt Elle reached over and placed a strong hand on top of one of his hands.

"You can *lead* only as far as you *grow*. And you will grow only as far as you let yourself."

"Yikes," said Ben softly.

"Yikes indeed," Aunt Elle agreed. "A writer I admire once said, 'I write to find out what I think.' Here's what I think, Ben.

"I think we *live* to find out who we *are*."

Ben closed his eyes, lost in a swirl of thoughts and feelings.

After a moment he opened his eyes again and said, "Were you going to say anything about the word itself?"

"The word?"

"The word *character*."

Aunt Elle smiled. "Now that you mention it."

A sip of tea.

"*Character* comes from an old Greek word for *scrape* or *scratch*. It came to mean 'an engraved mark' and, eventually, 'a defining quality.'

"*Character* is what happens when life scratches itself onto your soul."

"Claire mentioned that you love words," Ben said.

Aunt Elle nodded. "That I do," she agreed. "Words are the footprints of God."

Ben thought for a moment, trying to recall their earlier conversation. "Hang on, though. I thought you said, words were the greatest *human* invention ever."

Aunt Elle pushed her glasses up on her nose and peered through them at him. "That too."

Ben did not write in his notebook before going to bed that night. He was too wrapped up in thoughts and memories. He fell into a troubled sleep, in which images from his hospital visit that morning—and from other hospital visits long ago—pulled at him and refused to let him rest.

Finally, in the darkest hours of the night, he slipped quietly from the bed, taking care not to wake Melanie, and padded to his study, where he opened his manifesto and added another page of writing:

STAND FOR SOMETHING

Lead with your soul.

*What you have to give, you offer least of all through
what you say; in greater part through what you do;
but in greatest part through who you are.*

Competence matters. Character matters more.

*Character is what happens when life
scratches itself onto your soul.*

*You can lead only as far as you grow.
And you will grow only as far as you let yourself.*

11

ROBBIE

Saturday morning, Ben awoke with a renewed sense of urgency. The board-meeting showdown was just two days away. As he shaved and showered, he determined to put aside all thoughts of Aunt Elle, their lunchtime conversations about influence, and his "keys to legendary leadership." It was time to get down to business.

After breakfast he dove into his research with a vengeance. For hours, he pored through stacks of papers on Allen & Augustine—annual reports, marketing studies, cost-benefit analyses, and more.

He felt he had struck out with all four of the company's executives, and was no closer to securing their vote than he had been at the beginning of the week. Further, if anything.

But it wasn't over, not by a long shot. He hadn't gotten that reputation as one who did his homework and ran hard by sitting back and admitting defeat. He felt sure this merger would be in Allen & Augustine's best interests. And if it took him all weekend, he was going to assemble the data to prove it.

Come Monday evening, he would be ready—and he was going to take home the trophy.

Early that afternoon, Mel appeared at the door of the study. "Ben?" she said.

He looked up. "Mm?"

"You want me to take Robbie?" she said.

"Take Robbie where?" And then he remembered. Of course. Saturday afternoon. The tournament.

"It's okay," she said. "You should stay here."

"No, no, I'll do it," said Ben, getting up from his chair and stretching out his back. "I promised."

When Ben and Robbie reached the big gymnasium, they joined Robbie's teammates, who were assembling in one corner around their young instructor, Kim.

Kim congratulated Robbie on his black belt, and all the other kids applauded. Ben felt himself swell up with pride. His son—a black belt! *With honors.*

Kim invited Robbie and another boy to come up in front of the group for a brief sparring demonstration. The other boy was a head taller than Robbie—and, from the looks of him, a good twenty pounds heavier. Robbie put him gracefully on the floor inside thirty seconds. Ben was impressed . . . and intrigued.

It reminded him of his own confrontation with the big man at the café on Wednesday. Only in that encounter, it had been Aunt Elle, not Ben, who disarmed the bigger man.

Kim gathered the kids around for a pre-tournament pep talk. Ben had never really listened to these talks. On the relatively rare occasions that he was able to attend one of Robbie's events (nine times out of ten Ben would be at work, and it was Mel on "tourney duty"), he would typically be mingling with the other parents as they settled into the stands to watch.

Today, though, he wanted to hear what the young instructor had to say.

"Before we begin the tournament," Kim began, addressing the several dozen boys and girls on the mats before him, "we need to ground ourselves in the four pillars of our dojo."

Without further prompting, the kids quickly went silent.

"Pillar one: *mind*.

"The battle is over before either of you lands the first blow. It is waged first and foremost in your mind. See the entire sequence unfold in your mind's eye before you make the first move. *See* the other contestant on the floor, subdued and unhurt. The only question is how you can best help to put him there.

"Pillar two: *connection*.

"It is possible to fight a good match only when you *join* with the person you are fighting. Rather than seeing your sparring partner as an opponent to be beaten, regard him as a collaborator, working together with you toward a shared conclusion.

"When you put him on the mat, it is not that you have vanquished him, but that you have used his force and trajectory, together with your own, to bring about a harmonious resolution in which both of you emerge unhurt. *You* have triumphed and won the match—but it is a win that honors you both."

Ben was impressed that the kids were all, each one of them, in rapt attention, focusing on Kim's every word.

"Pillar three: *flow*.

"Don't overthink. See the match in your mind, but once you are in motion, let go and trust your training. Trust your instincts. Don't try to control the sequence of events. Let it unfold."

Ben suddenly felt a tug of familiarity. *Trust your instincts.* Hadn't Frank said something just like that? Or was it Claire? Or both?

"Pillar four," continued Kim. "*Honor.*

"The bow you make to each other before each match is not an empty gesture, and far more than mere tradition. Your form, your skill, your execution—these are all important. But more important than any of these is your *being.* By this we mean your sense of respect, as well as self-worth, of dignity and character. How you behave toward yourself, your opponent, your team, and your dojo.

"Mind . . . connection . . . flow . . . honor.

"Now, go, and fight a good match."

Mind . . . connection . . . flow . . . honor. Ben was stunned. The parallels were impossible to miss. What the young instructor had just described as the "four pillars" of his martial art sounded uncannily like what Ben had been writing in the little notebook Mel had given him!

For the next two hours, even as he watched the tournament unfold, he found himself walking through a mental review of the past week's encounters.

Robbie had an excellent afternoon, winning three of his four matches. "Great job, buddy," said Ben as they drove home.

"Thanks, Dad."

Robbie's reply seemed a little lackluster, and Ben shot him a sideways glance.

"You okay?"

"Yeah. I'm good."

Ben wondered whether Robbie had gotten hurt during one of the matches, or if maybe he was coming down with something.

"You sure?"

"Dad, I'm good." Robbie grinned. "I'm *awesome*."

Ben smiled as he drove on. His son had kicked some serious butt today.

Sunday morning, Ben attacked the rest of his stack of papers. As on the day before, lunch was a sandwich that by one o'clock lay half eaten on a plate perched on the corner of the little desk. By mid-afternoon he felt bleary-eyed and overwhelmed.

"Hey Mel," he said after hunting her down in her backyard herb garden, "let's get out of here."

"What are you talking about?"

"Let's go downtown. Let's go walk."

"Are you sure you have time for this?" she said. "You've got a big day tomorrow."

Ben shrugged. "I'm getting cross-eyed. Robbie's at practice for another three hours, and he's got a ride home. Let's go."

They drove into town, parked, and took a long walk by the river that ran through the center of the city. Ben remembered bringing Robbie here when he was little, to play in a nearby park. They hadn't been here in ages.

For more than an hour, the two strolled hand in hand, just walking and talking.

Ben loved talking with Melanie. Most often, she just listened to whatever was on his mind, but on those occasions when they had a good stretch of time alone together, time to really talk, she would open up, pouring out her thoughts and feelings on a dozen different topics, and it would be Ben who would do the lion's share of the listening.

Eventually, it was time to go home. As they wound their walk back toward the car, Mel lapsed into silence. Ben knew this look: she was mulling something over.

"What?" said Ben.

"Mm? Oh. I didn't want to bother you with this, especially with, you know, everything."

"Bother me with what?"

She stopped walking, so he did the same. She faced him.

"Robbie wants to quit the team."

"What?!"

"He wants out of martial arts."

"He *what*? Are you *serious*?" Ben stood stock-still for a moment, then realized that Melanie had started walking again and raced to catch up with her. "But . . ." His mind reeled, trying to grasp what she'd said. "Why didn't he tell me?"

"He didn't want to disappoint you."

"But . . . I don't understand, Mel, help me out here. Why would he want to quit? He's so good at this! And he *loves* it. He's worked *years* to get his black belt. This is what he wanted!"

Melanie stopped walking and faced him once more. "Sweetheart?"

"What?" said Ben.

"This has been great for him," she began, gently. "It's given him all kinds of confidence. I wouldn't wish it away in a million years. But I'm not so sure . . ."

She took both his hands and looked him in the face.

"I'm not so sure it really is what he wanted. Maybe it's what you *wanted* him to want."

Ben was thunderstruck.

They continued walking in silence for a minute. Then Melanie spoke up again.

"He thinks maybe he wants to be a chef."

Ben said nothing as he absorbed this last piece of news. As they walked on together, he thought, *He's my own son. How did I not know that?*

That night, Ben went into Robbie's room to say goodnight. "Lights out, buddy. School day tomorrow." He stooped and gave Robbie a kiss.

" 'Night, Dad," said Robbie.

"G'night, Robbie. Great tournament yesterday." He switched off the light and went to the door, then stopped and turned back to face the darkened room. "Robbie?"

"Yeah?"

"Your mom says you're thinking, maybe you want to quit the team?"

Silence for a moment.

"She told you that?"

"Yeah. She said you're thinking, maybe you want to learn to be a chef."

Another silence, this one longer than the first.

"Well, yeah, maybe . . . I dunno."

As his eyes adjusted, Ben could see Robbie lying on his back, staring at the ceiling.

"You'd be a great chef, Robbie."

"Thanks, Dad, but . . . I dunno. I'm just a kid."

"If anyone can do it, you can," said Ben softly. "You're one of the most creative people I know."

Robbie looked over at him with surprise.

"You really think so, Dad?"

Ben shook his head slowly. "I don't *think* so, Robbie. I *know* so."

Robbie turned over on his side, smiled, and went to sleep.

12

CHAOS

On Monday, Ben had no appointments with anyone in particular at Allen & Augustine. Instead he planned to spend the morning walking the floor, talking with some of the employees he had met the week before and meeting others for the first time.

His idea was this: he would get to know as many employees as he could, engaging them in conversations about how the company was doing and what each one thought it most needed to get through these tough times. He wouldn't be making his own case for the merger—at least not overtly. Subtle, after all, could be effective.

That was his plan . . . but it wasn't what happened.

Once he was with the people at Allen & Augustine, face to face, his strategy seemed to go out the window. Instead he found himself simply listening while they told him about their particular roles at the company, about what they did each day, about life at Allen & Augustine, and, to a surprising extent, about their lives in general.

He went into each conversation with the renewed intention of sparking a dialogue about what the company needed and planting the seed of his own viewpoint . . . but within the first five minutes, he would become so engaged in the discussion that he would completely forget his purpose for being there.

He started with the young man in Production, whom he'd seen Frank coaching on the fine points of woodwork detail. From Production he went to visit people in Repair, on the second floor, and then on through every floor and every department, eventually ending up on the top floor, where (along with Allen's office) the offices of Legal and Accounting were located.

There, while talking with a young man on the company's in-house counsel team about the adorable litter of abandoned puppies the man's son had recently adopted (Ben had read about this the previous week in a caption on those photo-gallery walls on 2), he noticed a knot of several employees huddled together on the far side of the office, speaking in quiet voices and glancing occasionally in his direction. After a few minutes, one of them, a woman in her twenties, approached him. She stopped a few feet away and waited until he had finished his conversation with the young lawyer before speaking to him.

"You're the guy from Marden?"

"Yes. I'm Ben."

"You the one who went to the hospital Friday?"

"Yes. You must be . . . Phoebe?"

The young woman nodded. "They said you sat with her for, like, an hour."

It was actually closer to two, but Ben just nodded and asked, "How is she doing?"

Phoebe looked away, then back at Ben. "She passed—that night." She managed a smile. "Anyway, I just wanted to thank you."

Ben realized she was holding out her hand to shake. He took her hand with both of his. "I'm so sorry."

———

At lunchtime he left the building and walked briskly down the block toward the café. Today he was especially eager to meet with Aunt Elle. It would be the last chance he'd have to talk with her before the big board meeting that evening, and he very much wanted to get her take on the approach he had developed for his speech.

When Sal ushered him to the corner table that had begun to feel like home, he found it empty. He was the first one there. *Good.* He could use the few minutes.

He ordered a hot coffee, then began going over what he wanted to talk about with Aunt Elle. He took out a business card, placed it on the table face down, and withdrew a pen from his jacket pocket.

The day before, he hadn't been able to put the "four pillars" of Robbie's dojo out of his mind. He had spent a considerable chunk of the evening looking over his jotted thoughts in his "Ben's Manifesto" notebook and thinking about everything Claire and Aunt Elle had said about influence during their lunches together. Before going to sleep, he had done his best to boil it all down into four words—which he now wrote down carefully on the back of the business card.

Vision

Empathy

Grounding

Soul

This, in extremely abbreviated form, was his outline of the speech he would give that evening.

A waiter Ben did not recognize came by to see if he wanted to order.

"Thank you so much," replied Ben, "I appreciate it. I'd like to hold off for a bit, though, if that's okay. I'm waiting for someone to join me."

"*Tutto bene*," said the waiter softly, and quickly disappeared.

Ben turned his attention back to his mini-outline and began reviewing his speech in his mind.

First, he would paint a picture of Allen & Augustine's story, from its churchyard days to its stunning ascendency, through its current troubled times, and on into the chapter that lay ahead—the exciting recapture of its former glory.

Next, he would put a human face on that vision, sharing a few stories of individuals at another company that had struggled before being acquired by Marden, and how the shot in the arm that merger provided had subsequently changed their lives.

Then came the *grounding* section—and this was where his homework would pay off in spades. He had *done the work*, all right: the vision he was sketching out was a tall order, but he had the facts to back it up and lock it down. The Marden Group clearly showed enormous strength in exactly those areas where Allen & Augustine had been most lacking.

And finally, *soul*: he would conclude with an impassioned discourse on how personally committed he was to seeing the merger work out in the best interests of all involved, and how he would not rest until that had happened to everyone's satisfaction.

The waiter came by again: did the gentleman wish to order perhaps an appetizer while he waited? Ben chose an item from the menu, and the waiter vanished again.

Ben pulled a sheaf of folded papers from his jacket pocket: his speech notes. He figured he could afford to review them once again while he waited. He reviewed, and waited, and reviewed, and waited.

Claire and Aunt Elle did not appear.

Strangely, the more he went over his notes, the less certain he felt about them. He glanced again at his little back-of-the-business-card word chart. It looked very symmetrical, clear, and logical.

His appetizer came, and he ate without tasting it.

An hour had gone by. They weren't coming.

He paid his bill and left the restaurant, but instead of walking back toward the Allen & Augustine building, he began walking in the opposite direction, with no clear idea of where he was heading.

As he walked, he tried to put his finger on what was bothering him, but the more he tried, the more his thoughts felt like chaos.

He walked and walked, his path taking him past all the city's most famous landmarks. He walked past the Liberty Building, in the heart of the financial district—the tallest building in the city—without even glancing up. He walked past the city's sprawling auditorium, where famous speakers gave talks to packed crowds. He circled back through the old garment district, past the offices of Rachel's Famous Coffee and the foundation where Claire worked, a squat little five-story refurbished factory perched amid a gentrified landscape of boutique grocery markets and loft apartments.

Ben kept walking and eventually ended up by the river, where he and Melanie had strolled the day before. All he could think about was Aunt Elle's question.

What did he really have to offer?

He had the vague sense that there was something beyond the four points he had listed on his business card, but he could not identify what it might be.

"It all makes sense," he said out loud, to no one but himself. "Leaders hold a vision. Leaders care. Leaders get their hands dirty and their boots muddy, do the work, and make the tough decisions. And leaders stand for something.

"It's about all those things. *But . . .*"

He stopped walking.

But at the same time, somehow, it wasn't about *any* of those things.

He looked around at where he stood. His walk had taken him to the little park by the river where he and Mel used to bring Robbie to play. His legs seemed to have brought him here on their own. He now found himself in the park's center, facing a statue of an elephant surrounded by four blind men all touching different parts of the animal.

He knew the story: each of the four would describe the nature of the beast based on what he could feel of it. One felt a leg, the second the tail, the third the beast's trunk, and the fourth a tusk—and, not surprisingly, they each concluded it was a completely different thing.

The statue had been commissioned and placed there years ago by the city fathers (as he thought about it, it seemed to Ben he remembered hearing that the Chairman himself had had something to do with this) to remind the city's inhabitants that when people held very different viewpoints on the same topic, chances were excellent that no one position was wholly right—nor wholly wrong.

The thought brought to mind a comment Karen had made a few days earlier. "They're good guys," she had said, speaking of Allen, Augustine, and Frank, "and they all see important aspects of the business. *Aspects.*"

He supposed that was exactly what these four blind men were

"seeing"—*aspects* of the elephant. But wasn't an elephant far more than the sum of its parts?

Ben thought about that.

So what was he missing? Aunt Elle had asked him what he had to offer the company. What was the whole elephant?

What did Allen & Augustine need?

Suddenly Ben heard an odd sound, like a subdued chorus of oboes in the distance, or perhaps English horns.

He looked to the left and to the right, but saw nothing. Then he glanced upward—and saw a long, slender V slipping gently across the autumn sky. Canada geese, arrowing their way southward as the fall cooled.

"Heading for warmer climes," he murmured. He recalled reading somewhere that the V formation gave the birds far greater aerodynamic efficiency, allowing them to travel great distances without tiring.

As he watched, the flock's formation blurred and shifted direction, breaking apart and reforming seamlessly with a different bird slipping into point position at the V's apex. Ben marveled.

How did they know how to do that?

The gentle honking continued, gradually fading as the birds made for the horizon. It seemed to Ben the most beautiful sound he had ever heard.

At that moment the city's clock tower tolled six, and Ben realized with a start that he'd better get going. He had a speech to give.

13

THE SPEECH

"Allen & Augustine has fallen on hard times." The slender man perched at the podium paused, and the sound system let out a crackle. As the weight of his first eight words sank in, the five hundred–plus people thronged in their seats held their collective breath, waiting to see what he would say next.

For all his gentle, unassuming manner, Allen was clearly capable of commandeering a lectern and holding a crowd's attention. Ben was impressed.

"Let's face facts," Allen continued. "The last three years have been brutal. You know it, we know it . . . and the bean counters at the Marden Group know it. The salient question is, where do we go from here?"

He went on to paint a glowing picture of the company's future, a vision of new generations of the city's leaders being fed, raised, and educated in Allen & Augustine chairs. He reviewed the epic gains they had made, the innovations others had at first ridiculed and then come to imitate, their civic and social impact in their community, as well as their commercial successes. Their current travails were cyclic, he asserted, not terminal: they had been through tight squeezes before and prevailed, and if nothing else the sheer weight of history declared that they would do so again.

It was stirring, the quintessential view out the top-floor plate-glass wall. Yet for all Allen's eloquence, Ben sensed, to his surprise, that the congregation was not entirely uplifted. They were inspired by their leader's prose and devoted to his person—but they weren't buying it, not entirely.

Next, Augustine lumbered to the podium, paused, and looked out at the room with an expression both sober and radiant. Just as Ben had expected they would, his first eight words evoked a stark contrast to the mood of Allen's.

"What can I say? I *love* you guys." The room erupted in applause. "And what's more important, I *believe* in you guys." More applause. He continued on in that vein, giving an impassioned homily on the subject of how much he believed in the people of Allen & Augustine, the miles they had traveled together as a family, and the many untraveled miles that lay ahead still.

As Augustine spoke, Ben noticed something he had not expected. Despite the obviously deep and genuine fondness everyone there had for the man, they were not altogether in sync with his message, any more than they had been with Allen's.

Ben noticed Karen sitting in the last row, watching the proceedings, her expression unreadable as ever.

More speakers followed, mostly expressing their undying devotion to the company and, not so subtly, their view that the merger would be a mistake. A company lawyer (the same young man whose son had just adopted that litter of abandoned puppies) reviewed their options, from both legal and personal standpoints. A representative of one of their top suppliers, who introduced himself (to much applause) as a devoted second-generation Allen & Augustine customer, told a charming story about his mother rocking to sleep her grandson—his own infant son—in an Allen & Augustine chair just the night before.

Yet Ben heard barely a word of it. As speaker followed speaker, he found himself unable to focus on what they were saying, riveted instead on what felt like the unspoken mood of the audience. There was an unmistakable aura of vulnerability in the room. He began to sense that, if one were to push on them, the people here might well yield and move in the direction of the push. It was an uncomfortably tempting thought.

Suddenly he felt a palpable crackle of electricity in his hands. It was raw power. In that moment he knew that when it came his turn to speak, if he chose his words well—and in his meticulously prepared sheaf of notes, he knew he *had* chosen them quite well indeed—he could very likely sway these five hundred people, manipulate their mood, mold them like clay.

The Ben of a week ago would be feeling an anticipatory flush of triumph. And the Ben of right now? He wasn't quite sure just *what* he was feeling.

The last person to speak was Frank. Standing at the lectern, the big man gave the distinct impression that he would rather be anywhere other than standing on a stage, but that he was here to do what needed doing. He spoke briefly, from the heart, and without notes.

"Look," he began, "you know where I stand. This is the greatest company on the face of the earth. If it weren't for these two guys, none of us would be here. A lot of us probably wouldn't even have jobs. Or anyways, not jobs we love.

"We're all part of something great here. Let's not screw it up."

He left the stage to the loudest applause of the evening.

Finally. Now it was Ben's turn to speak.

He climbed the three steps to the stage, turned, spread his notes out on the lectern, then looked out into the five hundred faces gathered before him.

"Well." He paused, momentarily startled by how the sound system amplified and distorted his voice. He glanced down to the end of the first row, where, off to the side, sat Thomas J. Bushnell himself. By special arrangement, Ben's boss had been granted permission to attend the meeting as an observer only, and would not be addressing the group. Their eyes met briefly, and the message was unmistakable: it was all up to Ben now.

"I met last week with your leaders," he began. "With Allen, and Augustine, and Frank, and Karen. I heard what they had to say. I listened to your leadership just now. And you know, they make a good point."

Ben looked down at his notes. They might as well have been in Sanskrit. With a queasy sense, almost like an attack of vertigo, he recognized that his carefully prepared speech, much like his carefully planned conversations with the employees that morning, was out the window.

He looked up again at the people.

"Yes." Ben nodded slowly and then added, speaking quietly as if to himself, "Yes, they make a very good point."

There was silence for a moment. Frank shared a skeptical glance with the person sitting next to him. "Here comes the *but* . . ." said Frank in a stage whisper.

But . . . this time, there was no *but*.

"As you all know, I represent the Marden Group. We have tendered an offer to buy your company. You guys are in a bind, and we have the resources to get you out of it. My job is to persuade you that we won't wreck your company in the process."

He paused again.

"A week ago, I came here on a mission to convert you, convince you—if necessary, to steamroll you. To dazzle you.

"But you dazzled me.

"You are amazing. Do you know how amazing you are? I've watched you for a week now. The way you look out for each other, care for each other. The way you treat your customers and your community. The purpose, devotion, and richness you bring to each task at hand. You're not just building chairs. You're building *life.*"

Ben felt his voice catch. The intensity of his feelings caught him by surprise.

"When I got here, I thought your slogan was corny. *We hold you up.* I was wrong. It's not corny. It's the simple truth.

"In a lot of companies, when they face tough times, what do you see? More backbiting, more internal politics, people circling their wagons to protect and defend their own turf. Not you. You don't do that. You hold *each other* up.

"I told many of you this week that I wanted to see you recapture your former glory. I had that all wrong, too. There's nothing *former* about it. You are as glorious today, right now, as you ever were."

He flashed on the case he had so carefully researched, the argument advanced in the pages that now lay ignored on the lectern. It was a good argument, and it all seemed solid, powerful, of genuine value.

But it's all *me, me, me,* he thought.

Would you lay down your life for this company? Karen had asked. Maybe not, but he was prepared to lay down his job, if it came to that. The clarity of the thought startled him. To see Allen & Augustine succeed on their own terms, without even the subtlest intimidation or manipulation, he was willing to lay down his job.

Ben took a deep breath, and let it out.

"Someone I respect very much asked me a question that has plagued me all week: What do I really have to offer you? What does the Marden Group have that you need? I've been thinking about that. And I think I know the answer."

He looked around the room. *Here goes.*

"Nothing. There's nothing we have that you need—not really. A cash infusion? Distribution clout, market footprint? Sure, maybe. But there's nothing we have to offer that adds to who you truly are."

Without looking, he could feel Bushnell's eyes searing into him.

"Oh, I have ideas. Even pretty good ones." He held up his sheaf of notes and waved it vaguely. "I mean, I think this merger is a good idea. I really do." He gave a thin smile, then added:

"But—"

To his shock, a ripple of quiet laughter whispered through the room. He didn't know quite what to make of that, and couldn't let himself stop to think about it now.

"*And*," he went on, "all that is, is my idea.

"Of course, we have money. That's true. And as someone pointed out to me a few days ago, money is the lifeblood of an organization. 'Money is where it all gets real.'

"I wonder, though, if that's entirely true. Some of you remember standing in a burned-out churchyard, penniless. And you remember what happened next.

"It seems to me, money doesn't build companies. Companies build money."

Ben paused in thought.

"You don't need us—at least, not critically. And I'm not at all sure you want us.

"I could try to paint a picture for you of how our two companies could work together, for the benefit of both. But I don't have Allen's vision. Or Augustine's big heart. And I'll never have even half as much hands-on knowledge about how your business actually works as Frank has in his big toe."

He glanced up and noticed Karen in her back-row seat, squinting at him with a puzzled frown.

"I could tell you all about who I am and what I stand for, what I see as the future of this company. *But* . . . that's all just *me, me, me.*

"And this isn't about me, or about Marden.

"It's about you."

He looked around the room, carefully avoiding eye contact with Bushnell.

"I came here with a job to do—to get you to say yes. I'm sorry to say, I've failed. And it's not just that I failed to persuade you. Truth is, I can't even say for sure whether you *should* say yes. In any case, it's *your* decision. And you're the ones I'd trust to make it."

He started to leave the dais, then had a sudden thought and stepped back to the mike once more.

"You know, that question I mentioned, the one that's been dogging me for a solid week now? *What do I really have to offer you?* It occurs to me that I just found the answer.

"Ladies and gentlemen, I offer you . . . *you.*"

The room was quiet. Ben gathered up his unused notes, left the dais, and walked to the back of the hall, through the exit, and out into the night.

14

THE CHAIR

"You can go right in," said Thomas J. Bushnell's secretary. "He's expecting you."

I'll bet he is, thought Ben.

When he had reported to work at the Marden Group headquarters that morning, he was told that Mr. Bushnell wanted to see him right away. And now here he was, standing in front of the boss's door, his hand on the knob, trying to get up the courage to enter the lion's den.

He slipped one hand into his jacket pocket to touch the piece of folded paper there. He was pretty sure he was about to be demoted back to Sales, at best, or far more likely dismissed from the Marden Group altogether. Possibly after a sound tongue-lashing that he hoped would not be too humiliating. Talking it over with Mel very late the night before, after that calamitous board meeting, he had decided that, rather than be fired, he would offer his resignation.

That was the letter in his jacket pocket.

He steeled himself, turned the knob, pushed open the door, and entered.

There was no one at the big desk. Looking off to the right, he saw the backs of three chairs drawn around the fireplace at the far end of the spacious office. One chair was empty. In a second sat Bushnell himself, and in the third, an elderly woman who turned as Ben approached—

And suddenly Ben realized why it was that Claire's lunchtime companion had looked vaguely familiar to him when they'd first met the week before. It *was* a family resemblance—only it was not Claire she resembled but his own boss, Thomas J. Bushnell.

Andrew Marden, the founder and patriarch of the Marden Group, had passed the company on to his *daughter*, Elizabeth Bushnell, née Marden . . .

"Aunt Elle?!"

"Ah, Ben. Please, join us."

Ben stood riveted in place just inside the office door, his mind as frozen as his feet. *Elizabeth . . . Elle.*

"You just put one foot in front of the other," Aunt Elle said, "and in no time at all you'll be right here with us."

Ben's mind was still reeling. "What?" he said, dumbly, then realized what she had said. "Oh—right."

He made his feet walk over to where the two sat, and stood by Aunt Elle's chair.

"Why . . . why didn't you tell me who you were?"

"Would knowing have helped you any?" she said. Ben thought about it. No, he realized, if he had known who it was he was chatting with all week, he probably would have been so nervous he wouldn't have been able to hold any kind of intelligent conversation at all.

"Anyway," she continued, "I didn't know who *you* were, either, not at first. And I generally try to stay out of Thomas's business. I'm an old lady now, with her own affairs to attend to.

"Besides," she added, "it wasn't about me. It was about you."

Ben thought about that for a moment.

"The less you say," he ventured, "the more influence you have?"

Aunt Elle inclined her head an inch. "Touché."

Ben was still grappling with the revelation of Aunt Elle's identity, his mind frantically rewinding through their conversations of the past week and trying to sift through the implications and layers of meaning, now that he knew who she truly was—her stories about her father (old man Marden himself!), about her son the boxer (his boss!), her business experiences . . .

But there wasn't time to sort it all out. He wasn't here for a reunion. He was here to face the music. He turned toward the other occupied chair. "Sir, I'm so sorry I wasn't—"

"I know, I know," said Bushnell. "Here's the thing—and please, sit, you make me nervous standing."

Bushnell tweaked his head in the direction of the empty chair on the other side of Aunt Elle.

Ben sat—and was stunned by the familiar, otherworldly sensation. This felt exactly like the chair he had sat on in Allen's office. No, wait: it *was* that chair. What was it doing *here*?

But there was no time to think that through, either. Bushnell was speaking.

"We were never going to go in there with massive layoffs, you know, break their company up into pieces, dismantle what they'd built. Allen & Augustine is a treasure. We only wanted to give them the ground and the space to grow.

"And we'd told both Allen and Augustine that. But we couldn't get them to believe it. We were the big bad Marden Group. We couldn't get them to trust us.

"In short, we could not get them to agree to the merger."

Silence hung heavy in the room.

Ben slipped a hand into his jacket pocket and grasped hold of his letter of resignation. This was probably as good a time as any.

"Apparently," Bushnell continued, "the one person who *could* accomplish that was you."

Ben's hand froze. "Sir?"

"We had a visit last night, here in the office, after the board meeting. A visit from Allen and Augustine.

"At the meeting, they told us, when you said, '*This isn't about me*,' it made them think. They wanted to come over and talk. They were here for two hours.

"They said they finally realized what the real problem was over there. They saw what had been holding Allen & Augustine back."

"Really!" Ben was so intrigued at this, he forgot to say "Sir" or "Mr. Bushnell." "Which was what?"

Bushnell looked at Ben. "Allen and Augustine."

It took Ben a moment to realize that Bushnell had not simply repeated himself. He was saying that the two brothers had identified *themselves* as being the prime barrier to progress at their own company.

Ben slowly shook his head. "I'm sorry . . . I don't understand."

"Here," said Aunt Elle. "Let me show you something." She turned toward her son and said, "Do you have anything I might write on, Thomas?"

He produced a small pad of paper and a pen and handed them to her. She took the pad and wrote a few letters on it:

LEAD

Then she drew two curved arrows, indicating that the L and the D were changing places:

LEAD

Underneath, she now wrote the new word that this change produced:

DEAL

"This is what happens to so many leaders and people of influence. Kings, presidents, heads of religious organizations and great corporations . . . It can happen to anyone with a following of any size or number. After a time, *they start getting it backward.*

"They absorb all that trust and faith, the sense of all those people looking to them for guidance, inspiration, and constancy, and they confuse the container with the contents. Do you understand what I mean by that?"

Ben was not sure he did.

"As a leader, you become the container of others' hopes. When we say people put their trust *in you*, that is exactly what happens. They place their hopes and dreams, trust and faith, even their fears, in your hands, because these things feel too fragile, too big, too important, too valuable to hold onto by themselves.

"You become the trustee of their intangibles."

Ben felt the gentle curve of maple spindles at his back and smiled. "Like a good chair?" he ventured.

Aunt Elle gave another of her faint Sphinx smiles. "Exactly. Like a good chair. You *hold* them. Believe in them when they forget how to believe in themselves.

"*But . . .*" she added.

Ben looked at her sharply. Did she know about his verbal hand grenades? Apparently she did. She was *having him on.*

"But," she repeated, "you are *not* their dreams, you are only the *steward* of those dreams. And leaders too often get it backwards and start thinking they not only *hold* the best of others but that they *are* that best.

"They start thinking *they are the deal.*

"And the moment you begin thinking that it's all about you, that *you're the deal*, is the moment you begin losing your capacity to positively influence others' lives.

"In a word, to *lead*."

Ben flashed back on his long walk through the city the day before, and his inchoate sense that he was not seeing the whole elephant, that there was some larger perspective missing.

He had the feeling he was hearing that larger perspective right now.

Thomas J. Bushnell spoke up again.

"The two brothers told us that when they heard you speak, it jarred something loose in their thinking. It made them wonder if maybe they were holding on too desperately to the company's reins, trying too hard to keep things the way they always had been."

Aunt Elle now chimed in: "They said that, perhaps, they had forgotten what the central word is in their slogan, *We hold you up*: not 'We,' and not 'hold,' but '*you*.'"

Thomas J. nodded and finished the thought. "The brothers said they realized you were right. 'It's *not* about us,' they said. 'It's not about the chairs, and not even about the people who make the chairs. It's about the people who buy our chairs, the people we hold up. This isn't our business, ultimately—it's *their* business.'"

Thomas J. Bushnell paused in thought, then mused, "As Mother says, the best way to increase your influence is to give it away."

He glanced at Aunt Elle, who gave a quiet laugh.

"My father taught me something," she said, "something I have tried very hard never to forget: *Whatever great parenting looks like, it is not about the parent.*

"Great teaching is not about the teacher.

"Great coaching is not about the coach.

"And great leadership? Well." She glanced at Ben. "You can fill in that blank. In fact, I believe you already have."

Both Bushnells, mother and son, ceased speaking and gazed into the fireplace. Ben felt the heat from the logs and heard the tiny *pop! pop!* of air pockets in the wood expanding and exploding. He had no idea what to say, or if he should say anything.

Suddenly Thomas J. spoke up again.

"Ben, your career at Mergers & Acquisitions is over. You're out, effective immediately."

Now Ben thought his head was going to go *pop!* just like a log in the fireplace. He had expected to be fired, but not quite so abruptly.

"I . . . I understand, sir." He began reaching into his jacket pocket once more. "I actually came here prepared to—"

"Good," continued Bushnell, "because we have something else for you."

Once again Ben froze, his hand on the letter. "Something else?"

"Yes. You've heard, I suppose, that the Allen & Augustine vote last night went well?"

"Sir?" Ben was floored. Went well?! Even given this bizarre account of the two brothers' late-night visit to the Marden office, he assumed that after his unexpected exit from the board meeting, the merger had been roundly voted down.

"Yep," said Thomas J. "First count, over eighty percent. After a few minutes' discussion, they requested the right to vote again. Second time, unanimous. The papers are being drawn up as we speak. Allen & Augustine is about to become part of the Marden Group."

Ben was so flabbergasted at this turn of events that for a moment he forgot all about what Bushnell had been saying about Ben's dismissal before he reported on the vote outcome. A loud *crack!* from the fireplace startled him and jogged that thought loose again.

"Hang on," he blurted. "You said you have something else for me?"

Thomas J. grunted in assent.

"The *yes* vote came with a condition. They wanted one thing. We promised we'd do our best to deliver it."

"Which was?"

"If they're going to be part of another company, Ben, they want someone new leading them. The brothers agreed."

Aunt Elle now spoke up again.

"The brothers also said they wanted to come over last night in order to bring something for you."

"Something for me?"

She smiled.

"You're sitting in it. The First Chair. That's yours now. And

Allen said to tell you this, that you'd understand what he meant: *Maybe*, he said, *it's time to move to a bigger building.*"

The First Chair? His?

"Close your mouth," said Aunt Elle. "You'll catch flies."

Ben felt the smooth wood surfaces holding him and remembered something Allen had said when they first met (was it really only a week ago?!) in his eighth-floor office:

The only reason we still have that chair is that we gave it away.

Had he been talking about the leadership of his own company, without even realizing it?

Aunt Elle reached over and patted one of Ben's hands. "Ben, you said you always wanted to meet the Chairman?"

Ben nodded vaguely, feeling as if he were in a dream . . . which, he supposed, he was.

"Well." Aunt Elle pushed her glasses up on her nose and peered through them at Ben.

"Now you *are* the Chair."

Ben's Manifesto

Ben's Keys to
Legendary Leadership

KEY #1. HOLD THE VISION

KEY #2. BUILD YOUR PEOPLE

KEY #3. DO THE WORK

KEY #4. STAND FOR SOMETHING

KEY #5. SHARE THE MANTLE

HOLD THE VISION

Lead with your mind.

Anyone can come up with a vision.
The hard part is the holding.

Building a business—building anything—is an act of faith.

Keep seeing in your mind's eye where it is you're going, even
when nobody else does. Especially when nobody else does.

Never forget where you came from.

And watch your personal pronouns.

BUILD YOUR PEOPLE

Lead from the heart.

Give people something good to live up to—
something great—and they usually will.

The more you yield, the more power you have.

The substance of influence is pull ... not push.

Tact is the language of strength.

And don't react—respond.

DO THE WORK

Lead from your gut.

Know your pegs and shims.

Stay hugely humble.

Get mud on your boots.

Stay grounded.

And trust yourself.

STAND FOR SOMETHING

Lead with your soul.

What you have to give, you offer least of all through
what you say; in greater part through what you do;
but in greatest part through who you are.

Competence matters. Character matters more.

Character is what happens when life
scratches itself onto your soul.

You can lead only as far as you grow.
And you will grow only as far as you let yourself.

SHARE THE MANTLE

Let others lead.

It's not about you ... it's about them.

Don't get it backward: don't start thinking you're the deal.

The best way to increase your influence is to give it away.

Sometimes it's time to move to a bigger building.

ACKNOWLEDGMENTS

When friends meet a newborn baby, what's the first thing they say? "He has his mother's eyes . . . Ohh, look at that chin—just like his dad!" As time goes by, upon closer inspection by those who know the family well, more ancestral clues reveal themselves: "See that impish grin? That's his mom's father . . . She's so creative, isn't she? I think she gets that from her mother's mother's side of the family . . ."

Books are like babies. Yes, they have parents, authors whose names are displayed on their covers—but their DNA is more complicated than that. If you look carefully between the lines and within the words, you'll find whorls of fingertips and tints of eye color that bear traces of great-grandparents, uncles and aunts, distant cousins, and all manner of friends and relations.

Among the tally of this book's hereditary strands, too numerous to catalog fully, our thanks go especially:

To Dale Carnegie, for his timeless observation, "A man convinced against his will is of the same opinion still."

To Joan Didion, for her marvelous line, "I write to find out what I think."

To Les Giblin, for the wonderful quote from Winston Churchill, and for articulating (in his classic *How to Have Confidence and Power in Dealing with People*) the idea of letting others live up to the expectations you give them.

To Le Herron, for his example and his inspiring story (which appears in his book *Making Your Company Human*).

To Tryggvi Magnusson, founder of From the Forest and real-life developer of Allen & Augustine's "cooking the wood" color process (though Tryggvi does not use, so far as we know, a "sophisticated, computer-programmable sequence of steam jets" in his process or, for that matter, any water at all).

To Margret McBride, for her gentle tutelage on the implications of personal pronouns.

To Dr. Robert McNeish, for his timeless and oft-quoted 1972 sermon, "Lessons from Geese."

To Betsy Myers, whose description of the "photo gallery" walls she observed on a visit to the Dallas headquarters of Southwest Airlines inspired the "museum of everyday life" Ben observes at Allen & Augustine.

To Julian F. Thompson, for his description of the ping-pong room at Changes, Inc.

And to the staff, owners, and patrons of the Blue Heron restaurant in Sunderland, Massachusetts, where good portions of this book were written over exquisite food (and *never* an overcooked fish).

As Aunt Elle points out, *pull* is the substance of influence (not *push*)—and among the many stars whose gravitational pull exerted its tug on the soul and sense of this story, our gratitude also extends:

To Margret McBride (yes, again), our legendary literary agent, along with Faye Atchison, Anne Bomke, and Donna DeGutis, who all believed in the colors and hues hidden inside the original manuscript of the first Go-Giver book and encouraged us to apply the heat and steam it took to bring them to the surface.

To Adrian Zackheim, our brilliant publisher, and Brooke Carey, our delightful editor, who both caught and held the vision of this book; and to Emily Angell, Maureen Cole, Jillian Gray, Natalie Horbachevsky, Will Weisser, Courtney Young, and the rest of the remarkable crew at Portfolio. Authors could not dream up a better publishing partner: you folks know how to *build your people*.

To our circle of early readers, whose Aunt Ellesque observations and critique helped to shape the path of the prose in these pages: Fiona Ashe, Anne Bomke and Donna DeGutis (yes, again!), Dixie Gillaspie, Josephine Gross, Michael Maher, Ana Gabriel Mann, Mike Rubin, Dondi Scumaci, Scott Smith, and Susan Wilson Solovic.

To Kathy Zader, whose multiple talents and generous spirit have helped guide and realize the Go-Giver enterprise at every turn, from its online presence to the organization and execution of our live events. To paraphrase Augustine, we often don't know if it's doable—but if anyone can find a way, it's Kathy.

To Zig Ziglar and John C. Maxwell, recipients of the first and second annual Go-Giver Lifetime Achievement Awards, who have never gotten it backward and starting thinking *they were the deal*; and to all the innumerable leaders who have served as role models in our lives as well as for the words on these pages.

And finally, to you, dear reader. Can we whisper a secret in your ear? Its title notwithstanding, this book actually *is* about you.

ABOUT THE AUTHORS

BOB BURG is coauthor of the *Wall Street Journal* bestseller *The Go-Giver* and its companion volume *Go-Givers Sell More*. A former television personality and top-producing salesperson, Bob speaks to corporations and organizations worldwide on topics at the core of *The Go-Giver* and *It's Not About You*. Addressing audiences ranging from sixty to sixteen thousand, Bob has shared the platform with some of today's top business leaders, broadcast personalities, coaches, athletes, and political leaders, including a former U.S. president. His classic *Endless Referrals* has sold more than two hundred thousand copies and is still used today as a training manual in many corporations.

JOHN DAVID MANN has been writing about business, leadership, and the laws of success for twenty-five years. As a high school student, he led a group of friends in creating their own successful high school. A concert cellist and prizewinning composer, he turned to business and journalism during the 1990s, building a multi-million-dollar sales organization of more than a hundred thousand people. In addition to coauthoring *The Go-Giver* and *Go-Givers Sell More* with Bob Burg, he is also coauthor of the *New York Times* bestseller *Flash Foresight* with Daniel Burrus and *Take the Lead* with Betsy Myers.

Come visit our blog and share your experiences with our growing community:

www.thegogiver.com

Are you interested in buying multiple copies of *It's Not About You* for your business, sales organization, school, nonprofit, or house of worship? You can receive special discounted pricing, great service, direct shipping, and more through Penguin's Business-to-Business Advantage program. The program allows your local bookstore to offer special discounted pricing on this book for bulk sales. Call your local bookstore and say you'd like to use Penguin's B2B program to buy copies of *It's Not About You* for giveaway or training.

—*It's Not About You* 978-1-59184-419-8 $21.95 ($28.00 CAN)

Also available from Bob Burg and John David Mann

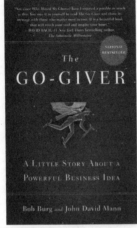

978-1-59184-200-2   978-1-59184-308-5

Visit www.thegogiver.com

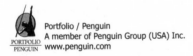